Calvinism and the Emergence
of the Modern World

"This is a staggeringly essential book for the church today! It provides the historical background and theological framework for Calvinism and its impact in the development and successes of modern Europe and the founding principles of the USA. M. Brett Callaway proclaims a clarion call for contemporary American churches to return to their heritage of a true, strong, and fruitful Calvinism versus 'the timid, fragile, sickly Calvinism practiced today.'"

—W. Sherrill Babb, president emeritus, Cairn University

"M. Brett Callaway's book is a timely call to return to the basics of the Christian faith, to an active, relevant Christianity much needed in today's society. His discussion of John Calvin's influence on the early Protestant movement and the continuation of that influence during the American Revolution and the founding of the United States of America should be a reminder to Americans to heed their own heritage."

—Ron Chapman, author of *To the James*

"M. Brett Callaway's publication on this period of history is a fascinating and concise read. The text cements the link between Calvinism/Protestant Reformation and the underlying religious current that led to American independence from Great Britain. No study of the American Revolution is complete without understanding the critical influence of the Calvinist theology on this era, and this book provides that insight."

—Craig S. Isaacson, vice president, Mountain Region, North Carolina Society of the Sons of the American Revolution

"I know well M. Brett Callaway's interest in and diligent study of theological history, especially the period covered in his *Calvinism and the Emergence of the Modern World*. This brief work provides a clear and connected introduction to the main personalities, ideologies, and influences surrounding this critical period in world (and redemptive) history.

To anyone who desires to understand more fully the immense influence of Calvin and Calvinistic thought from its early articulation to its seminal influence on the foundational worldview of early America, this book is a rich launching pad."

—**CRAIG SHEPPARD**, adjunct professor of systematic theology and missions, New Geneva Seminary

"This is a staggeringly essential book for the church today! It provides the historical background and theological framework for Calvinism and its impact in the development and successes of modern Europe and the founding principles of the USA. M. Brett Callaway proclaims a clarion call for contemporary American churches to return to their heritage of a true, strong, and fruitful Calvinism versus 'the timid, fragile, sickly Calvinism practiced today.'"

—W. SHERRILL BABB, president emeritus, Cairn University

"M. Brett Callaway's book is a timely call to return to the basics of the Christian faith, to an active, relevant Christianity much needed in today's society. His discussion of John Calvin's influence on the early Protestant movement and the continuation of that influence during the American Revolution and the founding of the United States of America should be a reminder to Americans to heed their own heritage."

—RON CHAPMAN, author of *To the James*

"M. Brett Callaway's publication on this period of history is a fascinating and concise read. The text cements the link between Calvinism/Protestant Reformation and the underlying religious current that led to American independence from Great Britain. No study of the American Revolution is complete without understanding the critical influence of the Calvinist theology on this era, and this book provides that insight."

—CRAIG S. ISAACSON, vice president, Mountain Region, North Carolina Society of the Sons of the American Revolution

"I know well M. Brett Callaway's interest in and diligent study of theological history, especially the period covered in his *Calvinism and the Emergence of the Modern World*. This brief work provides a clear and connected introduction to the main personalities, ideologies, and influences surrounding this critical period in world (and redemptive) history.

To anyone who desires to understand more fully the immense influence of Calvin and Calvinistic thought from its early articulation to its seminal influence on the foundational worldview of early America, this book is a rich launching pad."

—**CRAIG SHEPPARD**, adjunct professor of systematic theology and missions, New Geneva Seminary

Calvinism *and the* Emergence *of the* Modern World

From John Calvin's Birth through the American Revolution

M. Brett Callaway

Foreword by Bruce W. Gore

WIPF & STOCK · Eugene, Oregon

CALVINISM AND THE EMERGENCE OF THE MODERN WORLD
From John Calvin's Birth through the American Revolution

Copyright © 2024 M. Brett Callaway. All rights reserved. Except for brief quotations in critical publications or reviews, no part of this book may be reproduced in any manner without prior written permission from the publisher. Write: Permissions, Wipf and Stock Publishers, 199 W. 8th Ave., Suite 3, Eugene, OR 97401.

Wipf & Stock
An Imprint of Wipf and Stock Publishers
199 W. 8th Ave., Suite 3
Eugene, OR 97401

www.wipfandstock.com

PAPERBACK ISBN: 979-8-3852-1798-4
HARDCOVER ISBN: 979-8-3852-1799-1
EBOOK ISBN: 979-8-3852-1800-4

VERSION NUMBER 06/07/24

Scripture quotations are from the ESV Bible (The Holy Bible, English Standard Version), copyright 2001 by Crossway, a publishing ministry of Good News Publishers. Used by permission. All rights reserved.

Contents

Foreword by Bruce W. Gore | vii
Preface | xi
Acknowledgments | xv

1 Modern Points of Departure | 1
2 Dogmatics, Predestination, and Calvinism | 10
3 Calvin's Early Life | 22
4 Calvin's Personality and Initial Reception in Geneva | 29
5 Calvinism as a Force | 40
6 Calvin's Wandering Years and Return to Geneva | 51
7 The Rise of Puritanism in England | 61
8 The Influence of Calvinism in Scotland | 71
9 The Colonial Period | 82
10 Preparing the Way for the Great Awakening | 93
11 Liberty and Union under God | 103

Bibliography | 117
Subject Index | 121
Name Index | 123
Scripture Index | 127

Foreword

OF ALL THE WELL-KNOWN characters of history, few have been more controversial than John Calvin. There are millions who love him and view him as one of Christian history's greatest thinkers and influences. Others recoil at the very mention of his name! How can one man provoke such a range of reactions? Whatever else may be said of Calvin, he is certainly a powerful presence in history. The remarkable book by Brett Callaway that you are now holding pulls away the mist surrounding the name of John Calvin and exposes the remarkable contribution Calvin made by God's grace within the forces raging at his time in history.

Of course, for many the study of history churns up memories of brutally boring classes taught by distracted teachers whose lifeless questions about arcane dates and people tied heavy weights to already drooping eyelids! This prejudice sadly lies at the root of much of the poverty of historical interest in this pragmatic age. The antipathy toward the subject even among those who champion the historic Christian faith deserves both pity and censure, because if believers look upon the study of history as a waste of time, they may find themselves sawing off the branch upon which they claim to happily perch. If we implore people to accept a historic faith, while continuing to speak and live as if history is, at best, extraneous, what would we expect? We should at least feel uneasy that the Scriptures are full of historical information and strongly imply that we should make its study a high priority. In addition, it should go without saying that the history of God's work did not end with the death of the last apostle.

When it comes to the study of a character like John Calvin, the problem may be aggravated. The level of popular hostility to the man and his career may blind even more serious Christians to focused interest in the meaning of his life. In some ways, a prejudice against history, compounded by a suspicion of an individual in history, may lead to a misguided kind of study of the subject, with a risk of approaching the matter in a way that is too self-centered on the one hand and, ironically, not self-centered enough on the other. An objective review of Calvin's life will tend to free a person from inordinate self-centeredness, especially in a culture that revolves around smartphones and concerns that generally emphasize only what happens between our ears (or on our laptops). This attitude tends to abandon interest in the forces that created our world or turn it into a place where only the most banal appetites get the attention.

A study of Calvin's life confronts modern atheistic and naturalistic assumptions, and especially shows that the common outlook that history is generally accidental and meaningless, a mere collection of disjointed facts, misses the mark by miles. A study of the topic points emphatically to the self-evident truth that history has meaning, is going somewhere, and that a man like John Calvin had a great deal to do with pushing the story forward. There was a time, for example, when the proposition that Calvin was "the inventor" of America would have been widely accepted, but the idea would now sound shocking to many moderns. As someone once said, "An ignorance of history, and especially our own history, makes eunuchs out of men by cutting away any reason to study or believe anything."

To put it bluntly, our lack of love for history may reflect the fact that we are not selfish enough in our study! The stories of history should train us in how to live pleasantly and well. The life of faith is, after all, a good life. The Wisdom literature of the Bible affirms this; the Law commands it; and the Prophets thunder its truth. The great thinkers of history, men like St. Augustine,

Foreword

Thomas Aquinas, Martin Luther, and, yes, John Calvin, bequeath to us an incredible gift. History, in all its glory, is the passing on of accumulated wisdom and stories. These stories are our invaluable inheritance. They were bequeathed by our forefathers, not to burden us with long lists of irrelevant data, but to help us know our place, our people, our Lord, and, eventually, ourselves better. Any history that fails to help us tie the threads together and that fails to inspire a love of good things and good stories is hardly worthy of the name.

That is what I enjoy most about Brett Callaway's remarkable work, a book that corrects problems in our view of history generally, and our view of the life and influence of John Calvin especially. It calls us outside of our self and our age. It does this with solid writing and good analysis, but it delves deeper, unearthing the details of a particular man, because it is in the details of the past where we can mine for love and wisdom in the present. It is in the details of stories about particular people that we find the marrow of life and see the hand of God at work. It is by learning this we can both see and enjoy the history of the Reformation, and especially the currents that led irresistibly to the birth of the American nation. The worldview of this book lands firmly within the deep and abiding orthodoxy of the Christian faith, and at the same time beckons us to make application by winsomely shining the light of truth on these good and interesting stories.

Read this book and read it deeply. It will help you learn about God, your forefathers, yourself, and the world around you. It should help you to enjoy life, the word of God, and the remarkable saga of heroic Christians like Calvin, who informs and challenges us more deeply and fully in ways that we certainly need.

May God bless your reading of this volume and may that reading make your study of the Scripture itself more satisfying and richer.

Bruce W. Gore

Preface

As I write this today, America faces a number of problems, the roots of which lie deep within the soil of corruption. I don't mean "corruption" in merely a legal or even ethical sense, because law and ethics have their own roots. No, the corruption is all the way down to the core of who we are. And that begs the question "Who are we?" And, "What kind of world is this?" These age-old questions are no less relevant to today's practical and very real problems than they were hundreds or even thousands of years ago. We often smugly think we are beyond these questions. Are we? If we live in a purposeless world that is a result of random collisions of atoms that over time led to plants and animals, mountains and sunsets, closely interrelated biological relationships of organisms comprising complex ecosystems, and physical relationships of planetary systems comprising galaxies, we have no more reason to strive or love, despair or hope, than does a rock. In that context today's "problems" aren't problems. They are random, meaningless events, and we should give no more thought to the brutal rape and killing of a child by a pedophile than we would to dust being lifted from one place by the wind and deposited elsewhere. We should yawn at the claims of racism, misinformation, theft, murder, wars, human trafficking, truth, or any of the other issues we claim to be concerned with if, after all, they are random, meaningless events—nothing more. As a matter of practical fact, no one actually lives their lives as if they believe this. No one. Even atheists do not live their lives without attempting to direct outcomes;

Preface

they live as though outcomes matter and actions have purpose. If we were to encounter someone who made no attempt to influence outcomes affecting their lives, we would recognize them as being dead, mentally, spiritually, and, very quickly, physically. Even suicidal drug addicts who have given up on so much of life and have given themselves over to their drugs attempt to influence outcomes. Their lives are in service to the demands of their drugs. They do have a purpose, albeit a very perverse and self-destructive one. They do not rely on randomness to bring them the drug they so crave.

That leaves only one alternative—a world, an entire creation, that is neither random, nor accidental, nor purposeless. Every living organism by the act of striving for life is fulfilling a purpose. Lower organisms don't know their purpose. A plant that is cut back and resprouts does not do so out of any thought of purpose. Animals other than man lack self-reflection. They also strive for life. Higher animals like dogs clearly strive for more than mere existence. They seek happiness, for example, through affirmation from their masters. Man, because he does have the capacity for self-reflection, attempts to understand these motivations for life and happiness. It is from these deliberations that religions arise. Their beliefs are directed towards whom/what they claim to explain and justify their beliefs—their god or idol. The expression of their dedication to their god(s) is their worship. "Atheism" is a misnomer in that atheists worship a god. Theirs is self-worship. So their god is man. They claim to know enough to disregard the truth claims of other religions, believing their god is superior to that of other religions, thus elevating themselves to god status. Agnosticism is a variant of atheism in that it holds that man is capable of searching out and marshaling all the relevant facts about the great questions of life mentioned above and determining for himself their validity or falsity. It is a variant of atheism because it is a variant of man worship.

Other religions have other gods. They may be from nature, as with pagan religions. Islam's god is spirit, as are those of some other religions. The purpose of this book is not to argue the reality of the

Preface

Christian God versus gods of other religions. Rather, it is simply to acknowledge the overwhelming influence of the Christian God in America and Western civilization in general, highlighting some of its manifestations in the lives of individuals and society and showing how they have led to the rise of the modern world. We will trace the influence of a specific set of doctrines within Christianity broadly known as Calvinism, how those doctrines spread to early America, and their influence on America. I believe it will become clear how the application of the worldview formed by that set of doctrines caused America to become the greatest nation in the history of the world. By contrast, our decline has been a result of turning from these doctrines—because these beliefs have proven themselves to be most aligned to life in its fullest sense, including purpose, fulfillment of that purpose, and the happiness that comes from that fulfillment. The clear conclusion is that a return to the pursuit and application of these life-giving doctrines is the path to richness of life in this world and true life in the eternity that follows.

We begin with some of the points of departure that separate the timid, weak, increasingly irrelevant practice of our faith today as a result of changed understanding of its doctrines as compared with the robust, culture-changing understanding and practice for almost five hundred years. Then in chapter 2 we move to a brief consideration of the role of dogmatics to "mediate faith to its own true object: God in his living self-revelation. The better the dogmatics, the more it will be shown to hold up over the tests of time and even lead to a flourishing among its adherents."[1] Much of this book will demonstrate this flourishing over hundreds of years for the dogmatic system known as Calvinism. Chapter 2 also gives those key pillars of what Calvinism is from the standpoint of its concepts of God, man, and man as a part of God's plan and shows how these concepts that comprise the doctrine of Calvinism also determine society's expectations of government and individual liberty.

Chapter 3 covers Calvin's early life up to his initial arrival in Geneva in 1536, while chapter 4 discusses Calvin's life experiences and personality in the context of how he was uniquely equipped

---

1. Bavinck, *Prolegomena*, 39.

for the mighty work God had for him. Chapter 5 takes a brief detour in time, leaping ahead to look at Calvinism as the force it is before seeing its effect around the world in subsequent chapters. Specifically, it looks at Calvinism as both a moral force and as a political force. In addition to looking at it as a force, it is examined as a political system within the church based upon liberty from tyranny of men, because all bow before a sovereign God whose lordship is common to all. This church polity established expectations for how human governments should operate, including their limits before God.

Chapter 6 returns to Calvin's life and his time in Geneva, his exile, and finally his return. In chapter 7 we look at the kings and queens of England with a view to the changing fortunes of Catholicism and Protestantism and how these turbulent times gave rise to Puritanism. Chapter 8 takes Calvinism into Scotland, largely through the personage of John Knox. As a result, Scotland rises from a backwards and barbaric nation to one that has been credited with birthing the modern world. Chapter 9 follows the spread of Calvinism to America as the faithful risked all to come to the New World to freely worship their God. Chapter 10 looks at Calvinism in America leading up to the time of the Revolution, tracing the groups of "Old Lights" and "New Lights" and some of the leading religious figures of that time. Chapter 11 finishes with a look at liberty and union under God and how those concepts gave birth to the new nation of the United States of America.

Acknowledgments

I WOULD LIKE TO thank members of my Sunday school class for encouraging me to undertake this project. It has been a labor of love through which I have learned much. My objective is that it will be both engaging and informative to those who have an interest in history, the Christian faith, and how that faith sincerely applied in the lives of ordinary men and women is used by God to accomplish his glorious plan. I would also like to extend a special thanks to Bruce Gore for sharing videos of his teaching on the subject. They have been a source of inspiration as well as information. Even with the encouragement and support, the book has many shortcomings. They are all mine.

1

Modern Points of Departure

> The fear of the Lord is the beginning of knowledge; fools despise wisdom and instruction.
>
> —Prov 1:7

OURS IS A TIME that has been called a "post-Christian" world, even by some Christians. As a Christian, I consider the characterization ironic and impossible. Christ is King of kings, Lord of lords. He is the Alpha and the Omega, the Beginning and the End. The idea that God's creation can ever be "post-Christian" is arrogant nonsense. However, it reflects a pervasive attitude of the times. The fact that it is spouted from pulpits is indicative of the timidity of too many Christians. But we have not reached this point overnight; it has been a long road of many decades. And it has been the road described by C. S. Lewis in his *Screwtape Letters*—"Indeed the safest road to Hell is the gradual one—the gentle slope, soft underfoot, without sudden turnings, without milestones, without signposts."[1]

---

1. Lewis, *Screwtape Letters*, 61.

Calvinism and the Emergence of the Modern World

Yet, looking back, there *were* some signposts, overlooked at the time. Philosopher, author, and professor Olavo de Carvalho critiques the position typical of both the "post-Christian" mindset and the tactics used to bring it about. The National Bank of Ideas in Sao Paulo, Brazil, gave three alternatives in the evolution of thought:

1. Relativism
2. Skepticism
3. Established convention[2]

Notably absent was any reference to a religious or spiritual perspective, thus both censoring them as valid alternatives and implicitly classifying them as being unworthy of critical thinking.

Elsewhere Carvalho points out how this tactic is applied so that only three philosophies are considered by the intelligentsia as being among the accepted standards:

1. Skeptical relativism, which destroys knowledge and universals
2. Scientific relativism, which seeks new universals
3. Political correctness, which creates universals for political purposes[3]

Everything else is to be considered "dogmatism" and rejected as a viable philosophy.[4]

---

2. Carvalho, *Imbecil Coletivo*, 69.

3. Callaway, *Crossroads of the Eternal*, 73-80. I describe the systematic steps used by the KGB in the Soviet Union to overthrow a nation. They follow a very similar pattern:
   1. Demoralization—Undermining faith in one's nation
   2. Destabilization—Undermining the institutions of a nation
   3. Crisis—Creating an urgency to establish normalcy
   4. Normalization—Establishing new standards for society

4. Carvalho, *Imbecil Coletivo*, 70.

Modern Points of Departure

FIGHTING WHERE THE BATTLE RAGES

How did society arrive at this point? For two thousand years Christians have believed that God is Truth. Ever since Constantine, that has at least been the accepted premise no matter how poorly followed in practice. John Calvin's contributions brought about challenges to false presuppositions about truth, and about God-as-Truth in particular, to the betterment of mankind. Yet with steadily increasing prosperity, the vigor with which truth was defended became less until it has almost completely disappeared. We find ourselves today accepting patent absurdities such as men can become pregnant and have babies. With the rise of the modern world (beginning about two hundred years ago) the pendulum began to slowly swing away from the presuppositions of Christian truths and has gained momentum. The political movements of Marxism and communism and the philosophies of relativism, postmodernism, and now political correctness have relegated defense of truth to those who in the view of these movements are out of step with socially accepted norms, lacking intellectual nuance, or even to purveyors of disinformation. And the sad cycle common to fallen, sinful man repeats itself. We turn from God, fall under the oppression of tyranny, and are left to relearn God's steadfast love and our utter dependence on it. "It is good for me that I was afflicted, that I might learn your statutes" (Ps 119:71). When we understand the value of God's statutes, or presuppositions, we defend them. Francis Schaeffer says, "The flood-waters of secular thought and liberal theology overwhelmed the church because the leaders did not understand the importance of combating a false set of presuppositions."[5] He also points out: "The Christian must resist the spirit of the world in the form it takes in his own generation. If he does not do this, he is not resisting the spirit of the world at all."[6] For decades the church has been resisting the spirit of the world as it worked in previous generations rather than its current form. As a result the church has been feckless and increasingly irrelevant

---

5. Schaeffer, *Complete Works*, 1:7.
6. Schaeffer, *Complete Works*, 1:11.

against the spirit of the world. Martin Luther said, "If I profess with the loudest voice and clearest exposition every portion of the truth of God except precisely that little point which the world and the devil are at that moment attacking, I am not *confessing* Christ, however boldly I may be *professing* Christ. Where the battle rages, there the loyalty of the soldier is proved, and to be steady on all the battlefield besides, is mere flight and disgrace if he flinches at that point."[7] Unlike too many modern Christians who prefer to virtue-signal from the margins of the battlefield, John Calvin spent his life at those points where the world and the devil were attacking. His classic work, *Institutes of the Christian Religion*, is a result of a life spent where the battle rages. It gives us a system of biblically true and battle-tested doctrine. For the five hundred years following Calvin's life, Western civilization at least held enough of a belief in God and his truth to live and govern such that the human condition achieved an unparalleled flourishing even among the lowest levels of society, notwithstanding periods of regression along this larger trajectory of increasing prosperity and blessings.

GLORIFYING GOD AND BEARING FRUIT

At this point we need to take a detour to understand a point of departure between Calvinism as it was practiced for most of its first five hundred year history versus Calvinism as it is widely practiced today. It revolves around our purpose as God's creation. Our purpose (or "chief end") according to the Westminster Shorter Catechism is to glorify God and enjoy him forever.[8] But what does it mean to glorify God? The one place in Scripture where this question is directly addressed is in John 15:8: "By this my Father is glorified, that you bear much fruit and so prove to be my disciples." In bearing fruit we glorify God. And in bearing fruit we fulfill a direct commandment of God, "make disciples of all nations" (Matt

---

7. Martin Luther, as cited in Schaeffer, *Complete Works*, 1:11; emphasis added.

8. Assembly of Divines, *Westminster Confession*, 287, question 1.

28:19). So it is very important that we bear fruit ourselves and teach others to also bear fruit.

What then is meant by bearing fruit? Paul tells the Galatians (5:22–23) what the fruits of the Spirit are: love, joy, peace, patience, kindness, goodness, faithfulness, gentleness, and self-control. But this does not tell us how to *produce* the fruit. These fruits have become increasingly scarce in our divided society. What can be done to recover or even improve our fruitfulness? I believe the answers to this question are the crux of the divide between the practice of the strong, robust, fruitful Calvinism that formed the basis of the rise of the modern world and its immeasurable blessings versus the timid, fragile, sickly Calvinism practiced today, whose meager, flavorless, and deformed fruits have fed the spiritual and social decline now so evident.

Jesus gives us some strong clues as to how we should glorify God in the same chapter of John. He makes the analogy of a vine and its branches. Here we encounter other words whose meanings are essential to understanding what we are being told in the Scripture. Unfortunately, they have often been grossly misunderstood. They are "abide," or *menō* in the Greek, and "love," or *agape* in the Greek.

ABIDING IN CHRIST WHILE ENGAGING THE WORLD

"Abide" occurs ten times in the eight verses of John 15:4–11. It means "to rest, or dwell; tarry, or stay; remain; continue; stay; endure; to wait for; accept."[9] It would appear that by abiding we are being asked to be passive, hunker down, stay put, or wait. It is in this passive state of abiding that modern Christians seek to exist in the world. It is analogous to hibernation, that is, sleeping through a difficult season, or dwelling in a cocoon as an insect until it is time to emerge transformed. Reminiscent of monks seeking physically remote locations to live and worship, abiding in Christ is often

---

9. *1828 Dictionary*, s.v. "abide."

manifested in modern Christians by a withdrawal from actively engaging the world while turning to an evermore-inward focus seeking personal serenity with Christ as the catalyst. But is this a proper understanding of what it means to abide in Christ? Does it align with Scripture? I believe that while it does have scriptural basis, current practice falls far short of the fullness of its meaning; thus many Christians are misled about their purpose in God's kingdom. It has become a cop-out for those within the church, relieving Christians of the difficult task of abiding in Christ while engaging the world. For those outside the church it appears to be evidence of the irrelevance of Christianity to the personal and societal struggles we face in everyday life.

A much more robust understanding of what it means to abide in Christ is given just a couple of chapters later in John 17. It does not mean to withdraw from engaging and living in the world. It means that we are to abide in Christ *while* engaging the world. Jesus prays to the Father,

> Holy Father, keep them in your name, which you have given me, that they may be one, even as we are one. . . . I have given them your word, and the world has hated them because they are not of the world, just as I am not of the world. I do not ask that you take them out of the world, but that you keep them from the evil one. . . . As you sent me into the world, so I have sent them into the world. And for their sake I consecrate myself, that they also may be sanctified in truth. I do not ask for these only, but also for those who will believe in me through their word, that they may all be one, just as you, Father are in me, and I in you, that they also may be in us, so that the world may believe that you have sent me. The glory that you have given me I have given them, that they may be one even as we are one, I in them and you in me, that they may become perfectly one, so that the world may know that you sent me and loved them even as you loved me. (John 17:11, 14–15, 18–23)

This is the kind of abiding that is expected of us. We are to remain in Christ even as the world hates us for it. Just as the Father sent

Jesus into the world to confront the world with his truth, he sends us into the world that we may be sanctified in truth while abiding in the Truth, Jesus, as a result of being confronted with the lies of the world. We are not to withdraw from the world; rather, we are to be fruitful in the world while abiding in Christ for protection from the evil one. In bearing fruit we share in God's glory, his fruitfulness, as we abide in him. "The glory that you have given me I have given them, that they may be one even as we are one, I in them and you in me, that they may become perfectly one, so that the world may know that you sent me and loved them even as you loved me." We were tasked in Genesis to be the cultivators of life. True abiding in Christ is outward focused, away from ourselves, through Christ, to the world. Abiding in what too often passes as "Calvinism" today is inward focused, and therefore can't be Christ centered, as it claims to be.

LOVE

The other misunderstood word that forms a point of departure from true Calvinism is love. In English, "love" combines four different forms: *storge, phileo, eros,* and *agape. Storge* love is familial love, the deep, caring bond between parents and children, husbands and wives, and among siblings. *Phileo* is "brotherly love," like that among close friends. This is where Philadelphia, the city of brotherly love, got its name. It is used in John 11:33–36 to describe Jesus's love for Lazarus. *Eros* is romantic or sexual love, and is the only form of love that can be damaging to relationships if practiced with no boundaries.

"*Agape* love is the highest level of love referenced in the Bible. This form of love is everlasting and sacrificial, whether or not the giver receives the same level of love in return."[10] It also includes judgment and the deliberate assent of the will as a matter of principle, duty, and propriety. This is the meaning of love John uses to identify the type of love God embodies when he says in 1 John

---

10. Smyth, "Four Types of Love," para. 7.

4:8, "God is love." It is also the love Paul uses in 1 Cor 13:1–13. It is a description of perfect love, and is the same love Christ told us to strive for with each other in John 13:34–35: "A new commandment I give to you, that you love one another: just as I have loved you, you also are to love one another. By this all people will know that you are my disciples, if you have love for one another." Agape love has been defined as "the sacrificial zeal that seeks the true good of another."[11] It is totally centered on another, and sacrifice is required. It is also steadfast. It isn't ephemeral. We will see an example of how Calvin viewed and practiced agape love later in this book: he had finally settled into a very pleasant life and was asked to leave it behind and return to a very difficult and unpleasant situation in which he might very well fail. When contemplating it he told a friend, "There is no place in the world which I fear more; not because I hate it, but because I feel unequal to the difficulties which await me there."[12] And yet in a clear example of agape love for his God, prior to choosing the situation he feared, he said, "When I remember that in this matter I am not my own master, I present my heart as a sacrifice and offer it up to the Lord."[13]

Calvin's response is so instructive and so different from what love in practice has come to mean. Today's concept of love is to never make someone else uncomfortable by challenging their words or actions even if they are doing harm to themselves or others. This perverse concept of love is how we get the idea that "words are violence." It is what gives rise to "safe spaces" on college campuses where one is not to be confronted with an opinion that might make one uncomfortable. It underlies political correctness and "cancel culture," where people are no longer allowed to wrestle with challenging ideas of others. I can tell you that many of my closest relationships have come out of wrestling, even passionately arguing, with people with whom I disagreed at the time. Respect, even love, has often been the result of sacrificing or risking respect in the short term.

11. Tackett, "Tour 3," 24:50.
12. Schaff, *Modern Christianity*, 429.
13. Schaff, *Modern Christianity*, 429.

Modern Points of Departure

Fallen man will always drift from God without God's grace. God shows us grace by his revelation in his holy word, the Bible. God used Calvin to draw a few buckets from the infinite living waters of his holy word, as revealed in the Bible, and douse the flaming lies of the enemy. This book is a reminder of God's blessings to his people, those who seek to apply his word in their personal lives and in their communities and nations. In a plea for churches to retake their proper role in society, Eric Metaxas explains, "It is actually what we do that matters, because our actions illustrate what we actually believe. So if we do not do good works, we obviously do not have the faith we claim."[14] The present book is not an exercise in idolizing Calvin or Calvinism. In fact, there is very little theology in most chapters. It is rather an overview of how God has raised up nations through men who have been faithful to God's word. We need this reminder today when faith is again under concerted attack and at a low ebb in America. We need to look back and see how God has blessed men and nations who remained faithful.

STUDY QUESTIONS

1. Where does true knowledge originate, and how is it rejected by the intelligentsia?
2. Where must the Christian confront the spirit of this world?
3. How are we to glorify God?
4. How does the modern understanding of abiding in Christ hinder the accomplishment of our duty to confront the spirit of this world?
5. What is the proper understanding of the love Christ commands of us?

---

14. Metaxas, *Letter to American Church*, 60.

2

Dogmatics, Predestination, and Calvinism

And the high priest questioned them, saying, "We strictly charged you not to teach in this name, yet here you have filled Jerusalem with your teaching, and you intend to bring this man's blood upon us." But Peter and the apostles answered, "We must obey God rather than men. The God of our fathers raised Jesus, whom you killed by hanging him on a tree.". . . When they heard this they were enraged and wanted to kill them. But a Pharisee in the council named Gamaliel, a teacher of the law held in high honor by all the people said to them, "Men of Israel, take care what you are about to do with these men. . . . I tell you, keep away from these men and let them alone, for if this plan or this undertaking is of man, it will fail; but if it is of God, you will not be able to overthrow them. You might even be found opposing God!"

—Acts 5:26–30, 33–35, 38–41

Dogmatics, Predestination, and Calvinism

DOGMATICS: MEDIATOR OF FAITH TO GOD, ITS OBJECT

CALVIN AND THE DOCTRINE that bears his name have for the last five hundred years been brought before the world's leaders again and again to be rebuked and vilified, proving Gamaliel's warning, "If it is of God, you will not be able to overthrow them. You might even be found opposing God." In this book we will see many attempts to overthrow Calvinism. And we will see them fail time and again. For those of us who are Protestants, it is our heritage.[1] To the extent that we cling to its biblical truths and obey God rather than men, we too will often be held in dishonor for upholding the name of Jesus, and can rejoice in being found worthy of that reproach. Protestantism originated out of the Reformation as a protest against the doctrines of the Roman Catholic Church. Calvin systematized the Reformed doctrines of Luther, Zwingli, and others so that Protestant denominations are generally Calvinistic in their heritage and beliefs, though not monolithically so. By gaining a deeper understanding of the belief system, or dogmatics, we hold in common, we are better equipped for serving our Lord and Savior Jesus Christ in evangelizing others and disciplining ourselves in the daily practice of our faith.

Reformed theologian Herman Bavinck says, "The sole aim of dogmatics is to mediate to faith its own true object: God in his living self-revelation."[2] That integration of our faith with God's revelation to us is tested by the context of our lives as it was for Peter and the apostles. There are many denominations in existence today within Christendom because there are many systems of doctrine. None are perfect because they originate out of fallen, sinful man's attempts to understand and apply what God has revealed to us in his word. But some have been much better at withstanding the test of time than others. Some have failed, as Gamaliel

---

1. I understand that this statement may offend some who want no association of their denomination with Calvin. However, it is historical fact that Calvinism and Protestantism have been closely intertwined from the beginning. Subsequent chapters demonstrate this.

2. Bavinck, *Prolegomena*, 39.

predicted. Others are failing right before our eyes. Dogmatics, or doctrinal systems, that cannot provide satisfactory understanding of suffering, for example, will not last because they are not helpful to us in understanding our loving, holy, and omnipotent God in situations in which we desperately seek him. Leading up to the Reformation, the doctrinal system of the Roman Catholic Church had strayed so far from biblical truth that it had become a huge impediment to true faith. It was teaching many false doctrines. The Reformation was the movement through which God led his children back to him. Luther's Ninety-Five Theses were propositions that challenged existing dogma. This new dogma revolutionized Christendom because it was much better at integrating faith with God's revelation to us.

DOGMA

A dogma is a settled opinion; a principle, maxim or tenet; a doctrinal notion.[3] The word "dogma" has negative connotations in today's society, as it is often thought to mean a close-minded acceptance of certain propositions. Bavinck has something to say on this: "Dogmatics does not develop doctrine that we then have to accept with our intellect, but shows people how the word of God has to be proclaimed in order to arouse the listeners to a true faith and educate them to an interior knowledge of faith that corresponds to the truth. Accordingly, the sequence is: Revelation (scripture), faith, dogma."[4]

God expects us to apply that dogma to life. Bavinck points out that "religion is about practical experiences, about demands on the will."[5] Dietrich Bonhoeffer was another prominent theologian who understood that putting one's religion into practice by taking specific action in response to God's call is what is required of each of us. He was implicated in a plot against Hitler and the evil of

---

3. *1828 Dictionary*, s.v. "dogma."
4. Bavinck, *Prolegomena*, 39.
5. Bavinck, *Prolegomena*, 39.

Dogmatics, Predestination, and Calvinism

Nazism and was executed for it. He gave his life in the faithful, practical application of dogma to life. He taught, "The road to faith passes through obedience to the call of Jesus. Unless a definite step is demanded, the call vanishes into thin air."[6] There is never in this fallen world a day that goes by in which we can relax our focus on God's truth. Therefore, there is never a day in which we can stop thinking about the doctrines we hold to. Those that are sound, we keep. Those that lead us astray, we discard. Doctrine should always be tested by Scripture, not the reverse!

As the specific challenges we face differ over time, our dogmatics should reflect current circumstances without changing the fundamental, eternally true connections between faith and God's self-revelation to us. In Calvin's day anyone performing as a drag queen would have been burned at the stake in very short order. Any pastor openly admitting to being a homosexual would have been quickly and decisively dealt with. Today the church cannot and should not respond to such blatant acts of apostasy in the same way because of drastically different cultural mores in the society within which the church exists. But it should respond—decisively, compellingly, and faithfully. Faith and God's revelation must be integrated in a way that is understood by today's people but without compromising. The Reformers led a revolution against corrupt doctrine and all the obstacles to faith that it created. We need to do the same today. We can learn a lot from those who have gone before us in how we best serve our Lord today. If you are a Christian of a Reformed denomination, do you really know with any depth what your doctrinal system teaches and what God has accomplished through it over the centuries? In this book I will illustrate why Calvinism is the best option for addressing apostasy today.

CALVINISM AND PREDESTINATION

Calvinism is closely associated with predestination. For many, that is as far as their understanding goes because predestination is so

---

6. Bonhoeffer, *Cost of Discipleship*, 62–63.

often misunderstood. It is not my intention to cover the doctrine of predestination in any depth at all; there are many good sources for that.[7] Nor will I discuss TULIP, that acrostic so commonly associated with Calvin, but originating long after his death.[8] For our purposes it is enough to understand the basic pillars of predestination and how, both individually and as a whole system, they were revolutionary politically and transformational for individuals and societies in which they became prominent. Most importantly, and unlike any other belief system, they were and are revolutionary and transformational for good! Why is this the case? Is it merely due to evolutionary advantage attributable to a beneficial convergence of random thought patterns having no basis in reality? Even a cursory consideration demonstrates otherwise. Predestination is not a difficult concept, though. It consists of the following three pillars:

1. Concepts of God
2. Concepts of man
3. Concepts of man as a part of God's plan

CONCEPTS OF GOD

The two basic worldviews relative to the existence of God are: (1) he exists (theism), or (2) he doesn't (atheism). The leading argument of atheism is that we are here as the result of a progression of random events out of which we have "evolved." There are aspects of these two worldviews that are not entirely mutually exclusive. For example, a theistic worldview does not exclude certain types of evolution, such as occurs through plant or animal breeding.

---

7. See for example Berkhoff, *Systematic Theology*; Bavinck, *Prolegomena*; or Boettner, *Reformed Doctrine of Predestination*.

8. TULIP stands for total depravity, unconditional election, limited atonement, irresistible grace, and perseverance of the saints. Many of the denominational disagreements over Calvinism actually are disagreements with TULIP instead. TULIP was not developed by Calvin. It originated over fifty years after his death in response to doctrinal challenges from followers of Arminius. The points of response were formalized in 1619 at the Synod of Dort.

Dogmatics, Predestination, and Calvinism

Similarly, "atheism" may include views that are less absolute, such as agnosticism, that at least leave the door open to the existence of God.

However, the intellectual foundation upon which atheism is built is fundamentally flawed. That foundation is the theory of evolution. Its primary claim is that man, rather than being created by God in his image, is merely the result of evolution. Man exists as man as part of a long progression of random events acting upon prehuman species in such a way that evolutionarily advantageous traits are favored while evolutionarily disadvantageous traits are lost from the gene pool. Evolution itself has no purpose or direction.

However, this contention is refuted by its own logic. Disbelief in God is actually evolutionarily disadvantageous. Mankind, unlike other animals, is self-aware. We are able to consider actions and consequences over long periods of time. We are motivated in seeing that we have an effect far beyond meeting our own needs and desires. We even think in terms of "legacy," how our life will impact future generations. Will we be remembered for good? These are all concepts of man's purpose. With no God there is no purpose to our lives or anything else. Existence is random and meaningless. Any meaning we attempt to apply to our life, or the life of others, is therefore also random and meaningless. With no meaning in life, the will to live is diminished or lacking, and despair and suicide can result.[9] None of these things is evolutionarily advantageous. Therefore, the central argument of the atheist against belief in God and a purposeful creation, and in favor of organization and rule by

---

9. Atheist and philosopher Friedrich Nietzsche understood this very well and was honest enough to pursue it to its logical conclusion in his writings. His despair no doubt contributed to his going insane. This is not to say that there are no happy, well-adjusted atheists, or that all Christians are happy and well adjusted. Evolution acts through individuals on populations to shift frequencies of favorable alleles of genes in those populations. It is based on survival of the fittest. And fitness is determined under conditions of stress. "The blood of the martyrs is the seed of the church" is an adage that recognizes the fact that Christians have thrived under persecution ever since Roman times. Atheism ascends in times of prosperity, Christianity in times of trial.

"elites," is destroyed by its own logic. Disbelief in God is actually evolutionarily disadvantageous.

It can be argued that belief in God is evolutionarily beneficial. But is it real? I have elsewhere made the case that it is,[10] as have countless others throughout the ages. And having shown that the claim of disbelief in God and belief in evolutionary progression based on an evolutionarily disadvantageous foundation is illogical and foolish, I will not spend more time on God's existence. He exists!

Given that God exists and created all things, it is logical that he would have had a plan for what and why all things were created, and that he would be in control of that plan. It is an absurdity to conceive of an orderly universe that operates on natural and physical laws being created randomly and arbitrarily. And given the fact of natural and physical laws, we can acknowledge the Creator's control over his creation without having to understand every control mechanism or law. Boettner says, "To admit that He [God] has a plan which He carries out is to admit Predestination."[11] Thus, the pillars of predestination underlying the concepts of God should be quite uncontroversial. The fact that they often remain controversial has little to do with logic or science and almost everything to do with sin and our willful refusal to acknowledge God's reality.

CONCEPTS OF MAN

Malcolm Muggeridge observed that the depravity of man is at once the most unpopular of all dogmas but the most empirically verifiable."[12] An equally popular, perennially favorite corollary denying man's depravity is that man can save himself from his sinfulness. This of course makes the assumption that we actually want to be saved from our sin. This is about as true as a pig wants to be saved from the mud.

---

10. Callaway, *Crossroads of the Eternal*, 1–10.
11. Boettner, *Reformed Doctrine*, 21.
12. Zacharias, *Real Face of Atheism*, 131.

Dogmatics, Predestination, and Calvinism

The concept of man under predestination can be summarized in three statements. First, man exists in a fallen and sinful state. Second, he is incapable of saving himself from his sinful state. And third, all of mankind is therefore deserving of God's wrath and eternal judgment. These concepts of God and man mean that man has need of a Savior. Ephesians (1:4–7) tells us that God chose some to be saved and provided a Savior in Jesus Christ. This is how man stands before God as a part of God's plan. Entirely by God's grace, his eternal plan has determined that some would be saved from the fate they deserve and receive everlasting life in a perfectly restored world. If we were to have any control over that, God could not be God.

Boettner outlines the three main systems of belief regarding salvation.

1. Universalism. This holds that Christ died for all men, and that eventually all will be saved. This simply does not have scriptural support and has not gained any official traction among Christian churches. It is occasionally used as an argument against God's love or justice. But to use it this way, one must ignore or deny the truth of what Muggeridge said about the depravity of man being at once the most unpopular of all dogmas, but the most verifiable.

2. Arminianism "holds that Christ died equally and indiscriminately for every individual of mankind, for those who perish no less than those who are saved; that election is not an eternal and unconditional act of God; that saving grace is offered to every man, which grace he may receive or reject just as he pleases; that man may successfully resist the regenerating power of the Holy Spirit if he chooses to do so; that saving grace is not necessarily permanent, but that those who are loved of God, ransomed by Christ, and born again of the Holy Spirit, may (let God wish and strive ever so much to the contrary) throw away all and perish eternally."[13] It is a system that denies God's sovereignty and exalts man's ability to save

---

13. Boettner, *Reformed Doctrine*, 47.

himself. There are gradations of Arminianism in which man's participation in his own salvation is greater or less. However, in all cases man cooperates with God in his own salvation. It holds that man is not without ability to affect his own salvation. "Man therefore merely needs divine grace to assist his personal efforts. Or, to put it another way, he is sick, but not dead; he indeed cannot help himself, but he can engage the help of a physician, and can either accept or reject the help when it is offered."[14]

3. The third belief system regarding salvation is Calvinism. It "holds that as a result of the fall into sin all men in themselves are guilty, corrupted, hopelessly lost; that from this fallen mass God sovereignly elects some to salvation through Christ, while passing by others; that Christ is sent to redeem His people by a purely substitutionary atonement; that the Holy Spirit efficaciously applies this redemption to the elect; and that all of the elect are infallibly brought to salvation. . . . Calvinism holds that the fall left man totally unable to do anything meriting salvation, that he is wholly dependent on divine grace for the inception and development of spiritual life."[15]

Boettner points out the truth that "Arminianism is likely to prove itself more popular. Yet Calvinism is nearer to the facts."[16] We like to think that we have some control. That is a direct contradiction of God's omnipotence, and is therefore false.

CONCEPT OF MAN AS A PART OF GOD'S PLAN

God himself in human form entered the world he created and willingly allowed himself to be subjected to the evils and wickedness, the pains and sorrows, the temptations and heartache that are the substance of this fallen world. He did this to save some from the mess they had made of things, though none deserve

14. Boettner, *Reformed Doctrine*, 48.
15. Boettner, *Reformed Doctrine*, 48–49.
16. Boettner, *Reformed Doctrine*, 49.

such love. He did this because mankind is incapable of doing it ourselves. This salvation is part of his eternal plan. After creating the material universe, he continued, and continues, with his greatest creation, love. How can love be understood where its opposite never existed? What is gratitude where there is no need of sacrifice for the sake of others? Where is the sense of fulfillment when lack has never been known? Can there be a sense of purpose when there is nothing to achieve?

We cannot know God's mind. Therefore, we cannot know his plan for his creation in detail. But we can trust his promises and his purposes. We may not be able to fully explain the existence of evil. But we can rest in the knowledge that God works all things to the good for those who love him (Rom 8:28).

SUMMARY

The doctrine of predestination is much more than a theological concept. It is a system that integrates practical, obvious truths about man—who he is and what his life's purpose is—and the reality in which he finds himself. And it does so in a way that is consistent with those truths. Other systems are internally inconsistent and contradictory to a greater or lesser extent. One example of an internally inconsistent system is the belief in an evolutionary progression based on survival of the fittest, while also believing that an evolutionary disadvantage, i.e., random, purposeless life lacking any motivation to survive, is the driver for continued progress of self-aware beings. Those professing belief in God can also have an internally inconsistent system of belief. A very common example is Arminianism: that God is the Creator of all things and is all-powerful, yet has a plan that can be subverted by his created beings.

Need I remind the reader that these are the very dividing lines described in the fall of man (Gen 3:1-7), which pitted faith in God and his promises against man's ability to deny God and/or to become as God?

Predestination, as part of the system of doctrine called Calvinism, has often throughout history influenced society's expectations of government and individual liberty. If man is fundamentally fallen, sinful and unable to perfect himself, governments will inescapably be comprised of fallen, sinful, and corrupt men. They will inevitably drift towards tyranny and the usurpation of individual liberties. Therefore governments formed with this understanding of mankind are right to include checks and balances on power. They will look to God as the highest authority, above man and governments. Doctrinal systems that deny God and/or elevate man, such as communism, humanism, and monarchy, establish governments in which the highest authority are self-anointed "elites" who dictate what liberties others may or may not enjoy. The Bible is the story of mankind's rising and falling fortunes in correspondence with their adherence to, or denial of, the doctrinal pillars that were finally systematized by Calvin 1500 years after the last book of the Bible was written.

Calvinism revolutionized the world for the better across many nations and hundreds of years. Because society and government have drifted far from the pillars upon which Western civilization was built, we should be reminded of the doctrines responsible for freeing vast swaths of humanity from tyranny and poverty while unleashing innovation and creativity of a humanity liberated to pursue their God-given gifts. Let us now take a look at the man whom God used to develop this doctrinal system.

STUDY QUESTIONS

1. What is meant by "dogmatics" and why is it important?
2. How do doctrines prove their truthfulness?
3. What are the three conceptual pillars of predestination?
4. Boettner says, "To admit that He [God] has a plan which He carries out is to admit Predestination." Explain.
5. Compare and contrast universalism, Arminianism, and Calvinism.

Dogmatics, Predestination, and Calvinism

6. Why would a Calvinistic conception of man create different expectations about the role of government than would an Arminian conception?

3

Calvin's Early Life

> I know of no man, since the Apostles' days, whom I value and honor more than Calvin, and whose judgment in all things, one with another, I more esteem and come nearer to.
>
> —RICHARD BAXTER, PURITAN[1]

EARLY LIFE

JOHN CALVIN WAS BORN on July 10, 1509, in the city of Noyon, France, twenty-five years after the other great Reformers Martin Luther and Huldrych Zwingli. Noyon was an ancient city even at that time and was known as "Noyon of the Saints" because of its many churches, convents, priests, monks, and cathedral. Calvin's father Gerard Cauvin held a prominent position of apostolic secretary for the bishop of Noyon, as well as being the financial procurator for the county. Because of his father's position, John Calvin grew up in comfortable circumstances among the most influential families in the city. However, his father became involved in a financial embarrassment and was also excommunicated for heresy.

---

1. Schaff, *Modern Christianity*, 287.

Calvin's mother, Jeanne Lefranc, was beautiful and pious but died while John was still quite young. Calvin had four brothers, two of whom died young, and two sisters. His oldest brother Charles was chaplain of the cathedral and curé of Roupy, but became a heretic or infidel and was excommunicated. In those days being considered a heretic was often due to disagreement with the doctrines of the Roman Catholic Church. His younger brother Antoine was chaplain at Tournerolle. He and John's sister Marie became disciples of the evangelical faith and followed John to Geneva in 1536. His other sister remained a Roman Catholic and stayed in Noyon. Because of his father's connections, John was appointed to the chaplaincy at the cathedral of Noyon at the age of twelve! This enabled him to begin his studies at the age of fourteen. He studied under some of the best teachers available. In fact, one of his famous teachers also taught Ignatius Loyola at about the same time as Calvin. Calvin's studies continued at the best French universities in Orleans, Bourges, and Paris. He began studying for the priesthood but, due to his father's wishes, switched to law, which would give him better financial prospects. His father died in 1531, two years before John finished his studies. After his father's death, he turned to the study of the humanities and finally to theology. He was always an outstanding student, very serious and dedicated, but there was no indication until his studies were almost complete of the great reforming work that God would have him do. His first exposure to the public had nothing to do with Christianity. It was a commentary on one of Seneca's books.

CONVERSION AND EXILE

Calvin's conversion to Protestantism came suddenly in late 1532. He credits no human agency for it, saying, "God himself produced the change. He instantly subdued my heart to obedience."[2] At the beginning of Calvin's final year at university, 1533, the new rector, a close friend of Calvin named Nicolas Cop, gave the inaugural

2. Schaff, *Modern Christianity*, 310.

address. It is generally, though not universally, said that Cop had asked Calvin to prepare the address for him. In any event, it was like gas on a fire: explosive! It was a frontal attack against the scholastic theologians of the day. In part it said, "They teach nothing of faith, nothing of the love of God, nothing of the remission of sins, nothing of grace, nothing of justification; or if they do so, they pervert and undermine it all by their laws and sophistries. I beg you, who are here present, not to tolerate any longer these heresies and abuses."[3] Cop was able to escape the aftermath by fleeing to Basel, Switzerland. It is said that Calvin escaped police search of his quarters by descending out a window "by means of sheets, and escaped from Paris in the garb of a vine-dresser with a hoe upon his shoulder."[4] All his books and papers were seized by the police. As serious as that was, things might have settled down except that a man named Feret placarded another inflammatory tract against the "popish mass" all over Paris, including the door of the king's residence. It denounced cardinals, bishops, priests, and monks as hypocrites and servants of the antichrist. The response was quick and severe. In Paris the king himself led a procession of dignitaries to Mass. That was followed by public torture and burning of six Protestants. The blowback against Protestants spread to other cities over the next few months, leading to twenty-four additional public burnings and many more Protestants being fined, imprisoned, and tortured. Among those burned alive was a close personal friend of Calvin named Etienne de la Forge. Many others had to flee the country, including Calvin, who made his way to Basel, Switzerland, and took the name "Martinus Lucianus." It is interesting given the attempts today to label evangelical Christians as domestic terrorists, to note biographer Alister McGrath's observation, "To be an evangelical was perceived to be a subversive, perhaps even a traitor."[5] This accusation was deeply offensive to Calvin. He could not abide the claim that Evangelicals had political rather than religious motives. In response he wrote a book and

3. Schaff, *Modern Christianity*, 318.
4. Schaff, *Modern Christianity*, 319.
5. McGrath, *Life of John Calvin*, 74.

Calvin's Early Life

published it in August of 1535. That book was the first edition of his famous *Institutes of the Christian Religion*. It was intended "to discredit those who, for political purposes, sought to portray them as heretical and radical."[6]

Calvin spent the years of 1533–36 more or less unsettled. He spent much of the time in Basel. He also spent a few months in the court of the duchess of Renata in Ferrara, Italy. The duchess was friends with the French protector of the Reformation, Queen Marguerite, and became a strong protector of the Reformation in her own right. During this time Calvin briefly returned to his hometown of Noyon to settle family affairs before returning to Basel, intending to settle down to a quiet life as an academic. However, due to the dangerous times, he had to take an indirect route through Geneva on his way. He arrived in Geneva in July of 1536 with the intention of staying only one night. But God had other plans for him!

SWITZERLAND PRIOR TO CALVIN

The area surrounding today's Geneva was originally governed by a bishop and a count. They were very corrupt, as were many during this time under the very corrupt Pope Leo X. A patriotic party sprang up to resist. They became known by the Swiss German word for Confederates, which is Eignots. Over time, Eignots was mispronounced as Huguenots, whom we know as French Protestants. But until after the Reformation this term had no religious connotation. These patriots won the rebellion and formed a political and military alliance among Freiburg (which later withdrew), Bern, and Geneva. The alliance was to preserve political and religious freedom from Rome. It was a time when winds of the Reformation were just coming to this area. Bern embraced Reformation ideas two years after the successful liberation by the alliance in 1528. A man known as the pioneer of Protestantism in western Switzerland, and also as "the Elijah of the French

---

6. McGrath, *Life of John Calvin*, 77.

Reformation," was William Farel. He preached with great intensity as the fighter that he was. He was small in stature and feeble in appearance, but utterly fearless. In one instance, he was shot at, but the gun burst. He promptly turned around and said, "I'm not afraid of your shots."[7] He was also poisoned, but survived. He traveled widely, preaching indoors and out. "Wherever he went," says church historian Philip Schaff, "he stirred up all the forces of the people, and made them take sides for or against the new gospel."[8] He went to Geneva in 1532 at the encouragement of Zwingli and there met Calvin's cousin, Olivetan. The Genevans had gained their freedom from the Catholic Church, but had traded liberty for license. Schaff gives this assessment: "Geneva needed first of all a strong moral government on the doctrinal basis of the evangelical Reformation. The Genevese were a light-hearted, joyous people, fond of public amusements, dancing, singing, masquerades and revelries. Reckless gambling, drunkenness, adultery, blasphemy, and all sorts of vice abounded. Prostitution was sanctioned by the authority of the State and superintended by a woman called the Queen of the Brothel."[9]

That was the state of things when Calvin arrived in 1536 for a stay of one night. Farel learned that he was in town, believed it was providential, and insisted that he stay. Calvin protested with many excuses—his youth, his inexperience, the fact that he needed further study, his timidity, and so forth. Farel was having none of it! He threatened Calvin with a curse from Almighty God if he preferred his studies to the work of the Lord, and his own interest to the cause of Christ. Farel knew instinctively where Calvin was most vulnerable and appealed to his sense of duty and obedience to God. It worked! Calvin stayed. Like John the Baptist, or perhaps a better analogy would be like carpet-bombing before the ground troops invade, Farel had prepared the way.

---

7. Schaff, *Modern Christianity*, 237.
8. Schaff, *Modern Christianity*, 242.
9. Schaff, *Modern Christianity*, 353.

APPLICATION TO TODAY

I'd like to close this chapter with an application from today. As I was writing about Geneva and how the lack of good doctrine and discipline had left them very vulnerable, someone sent me an article from the *Aquila Report* that seemed very timely. The Presbyterian Church in America (PCA) denomination is considered to be a conservative denomination. As with all denominations there is constant pressure from the surrounding culture to become more like it. In this particular case a PCA church had left the denomination due to their belief that homosexuals should be able to hold office and even preach. This position was condemned by the General Assembly (the highest ruling body of the PCA), not to mention by God's word. In response, someone wrote an article about how sad it was to see the church leave. The article that came to me was a response to that sentiment. It contrasted two polar-opposite reasons for being sad. There was the response that was sympathetic to the offender, allowing "wrongdoers to depart imagining themselves as victims rather than perpetrators."[10] The author gave a number of examples from the offending church, including holding plays on church property celebrating transsexuality, and numerous instances of gross and gratuitous vulgarities from the pulpit, not to mention the initial violation of the pastor proclaiming himself to be homosexual.

The opposite reason for sadness was that discipline calling out these and other offenses to God was very late in coming and left the door open for the offending pastor to "publicly present himself as 'exonerated' of wrong and thus imply his opponents are slanderers."[11] This is where so many denominations are today and where Geneva was before Calvin. If blatant, proud sin is called out at all, it is timid, mealy mouthed, and devoid of the bold, unabashed, powerful, and steadfast proclamation of the fact of its sinfulness and rebellion against God. It also needs to be made crystal clear to the guilty parties that their sin harms themselves

10. Hervey, "On Sadness in PCA," para. 14.
11. Hervey, "On Sadness in PCA," para. 14.

and others, and how it is harmful. The genius of Calvin was in his ability to do these things and to do them in a way that showed the interconnectedness of God's word, sin's rebellion against it, and practical consequences in society. As we will see in future chapters, by demonstrating this interconnectivity, society has been able to formulate methods of government that take man's sinful heart into account with checks and balances and that recognize that our liberties come from God rather than government. This has reshaped civilization worldwide. And it all started in Geneva.

STUDY QUESTIONS

1. How did Calvin's conversion to Protestantism come about?
2. What prompted Calvin to flee France?
3. What motivated Calvin to first write his famous *Institutes of the Christian Religion*?
4. Who was known as "the Elijah of the French Reformation" and what was his initial meeting like with Calvin?

4

Calvin's Personality and Initial Reception in Geneva

> Now the law came in to increase the trespass, but where sin increased, grace abounded all the more, so that, as sin reigned in death, grace also might reign through righteousness leading to eternal life through Jesus Christ our Lord. What shall we say then? Are we to continue in sin that grace may abound? By no means!
>
> —Rom 5:20—6:2a

AT THE END OF our last chapter we got a view of the state of Geneva when Calvin first arrived. It was much as Paul describes in the verses from the book of Romans quoted above, licentious, full of the usual human vices, and having little inclination to change, but claiming at least some faith. Calvin was on his way to Basel, but as the Lord would have it, the most direct way was too dangerous to take, and the safer route took him through Geneva. He had planned to stay only one night before moving on, but as we have seen, William Farel convinced him to stay.

Calvinism and the Emergence of the Modern World

CALVIN: THE MAN AND THE MYTH

Calvin is known as a dour, joyless person, perhaps coldhearted, only busying himself in his work and pointing out the sins of others. Is this a fair stereotype? As in most stereotypes there is a certain amount of truth or it would not be an effective stereotype. There is no denying Calvin was much more reserved than Luther, for example. He did not bring attention to himself. In fact, even the place where he is buried is not certain. What is believed to be his grave has only a very simple headstone, just as he would have wanted. Duty was very important to him. He showed no interest in accumulating money. For many years he lived very frugally. When friends or benefactors offered him financial help, he often turned it down, accepting only if truly needed.

Calvin had an amazing work ethic. His close friend Theodore Beza described his ordinary labors this way: "During the week he preached every alternate, and lectured every third day; on Thursday he presided in the meetings of Presbytery; and on Friday he expounded the Scripture in the assembly.... He illustrated several sacred books with most learned commentaries, besides answering the enemies of religion and maintaining an extensive correspondence on matters of great importance. Anyone who reads these attentively, will be astonished how one little man could be fit for labors so numerous and great."[1] And one could add that he did these things at a very young age for such profound work. Luther and Zwingli, who were also very prodigious workers, were of better health and physical stature and enjoyed diversions. Luther had an almost playful relationship with his wife, and did play with his children. He also enjoyed entertaining guests around his table. Zwingli wrote poetry and played music. Calvin had none of these kinds of diversions. His exercise and recreation consisted of a quarter- or half-hour walk in his room, or sometimes the garden after meals. He slept very little and for at least ten years ate only one meal a day. When he was sick, he would dictate his writings from bed.

---

1. Schaff, *Modern Christianity*, 445–46.

Calvin's Personality and Initial Reception in Geneva

Calvin was a devoted defender of God's honor, and it is said that he loved truth and consistency more than peace and unity.[2] He had a long and deep friendship with German Reformer Philip Melanchthon, who was a very different personality. Melanchthon was always looking to maintain peace, often even if it meant giving a timid defense of certain points of doctrine. Calvin's relationship with Melanchthon was such that even when he strongly disagreed with Melanchthon's response to an issue, he always replied with the utmost respect and gentleness, while still remaining firm. On one occasion Calvin gave a very revealing illustration of why he felt as he did. Referring to how Paul responded to a controversy in Gal 2:5,[3] he said, "He boasts that they did not yield to them,—no, not for an hour,—that the truth of God might remain intact among the Gentiles." Then he added, "The trepidation of a general is more dishonorable than the flight of a whole herd of private soldiers.... You alone, by only giving way a little, will cause more complaints and sighs than a hundred ordinary individuals by open desertion."[4]

What is not well known about Calvin is that he combined these traits with a deep caring for others. He married a widow and member of his church named Idelette Stordeur de Bure, who brought with her several children. She and Calvin were very happily married and had a son together, who died in infancy in 1542. Calvin found comfort during his loss through the close bonds he felt for those in his congregation and beyond whom he considered his spiritual children. In a private letter to his close friend Viret, he wrote, "The Lord has dealt us a severe blow in taking from us our infant son; but it is our Father who knows what is best for his children. God has given me a little son, and taken him away; but I have myriads of children in the whole Christian world."[5] When Idelette died after only nine years of marriage, Calvin was devastated. He again wrote Viret, "Had not a powerful self-control, therefore, been vouchsafed to me, I could not have borne up so

---

2. Schaff, *Modern Christianity*, 382.
3. The controversy was over whether or not circumcision was required.
4. Schaff, *Modern Christianity*, 395.
5. Schaff, *Modern Christianity*, 420.

long. And truly mine is no common source of grief. I have been bereaved of the best companion of my life."[6] He had a pastor's heart, too, as his letters are filled with deep concern and compassion for those in his flock and in his wide correspondence. Because these were private, this side of Calvin isn't well known or appreciated. He brought all these traits to Geneva and applied them, while teaching their biblical basis. These characteristics also are apparent in his extremely influential *Institutes* and other writings.

PERSONALITY PROFILE OF CALVINISM

What later became known as Calvinism is a system of doctrine that has what could also be described as a personality profile. It is a demonstration of God's will for us as reflected through a particular personality type. And Calvin was uniquely suited by God's grace to fulfill this role. Luther's personality demonstrated other aspects of God's will for us. We are each uniquely designed by God to reflect his will for mankind to those whom we influence. It is through the expression of our faith in the situations in which God places us that this influence occurs. God blessed Calvin with the traits he did and placed him in the circumstances he did in order that through faith he might have a large role in God's plan. We also are more or less successful in fulfilling God's purpose for us by our fidelity to his word. And our actions may influence those that witness them.

Think of Jesus's temptation in the wilderness (Luke 4:1–13). Satan tempted Jesus to use his influence in ways that would not be pleasing to God the Father. As with all temptations, they appealed to selfish motivations. It is possible to see another subtlety about this exchange with Satan. It seems Satan chose these particular temptations because each specifically targeted a different motivator. Jesus had not eaten for forty days. The temptation to turn rocks to bread was one very specifically targeted to satisfy *self*. The temptation for authority over all the kingdoms of the world was more

---

6. Schaff, *Modern Christianity*, 419.

Calvin's Personality and Initial Reception in Geneva

directed towards duty, or benefit to *others*, of course still through an egotistical lens. And the third temptation was pointed more directly towards trust in *God's* promises, questioning his faithful protection of his children, in this case the protection of Jesus from physical harm if he fell.

Calvin's personality was unusually strong in three areas: First, his selflessness. Second, he had an enormously strong sense of duty to others. And third was his sense of obedience to God. He had other commendable traits—his kindness to his friends and congregants, for example. But if asked to describe the practice of Calvinism in a few words, "selfless duty in obedience to God" would not be a bad choice. Calvinism, when it is rightly practiced, has been powerfully transformative because of its attention to these three areas. Why? These three areas cover the three kinds of relationships, or one could say, our three types of knowledge in which we live: our relationship to ourselves, to others, and to God. Calvin begins his *Institutes* by saying, "Without knowledge of self there is no knowledge of God. Nearly all of the wisdom we possess, that is, true sound wisdom, consists of two parts: knowledge of God and of ourselves."[7] The late Reformed Theological Seminary theologian Knox Chamblin rightfully extends this to include a third part—others.[8] We grow in our sanctification as human beings through a never-ending iterative cycle of feedback and response as we live and move in these three relationships. But the feedback must be continually placed in the context of God's word. The cycle is broken and the opportunity is lost whenever we try to place those relationships into any other context. God's being is a Trinity of perfect relationships that, as his image bearers, we are to reflect. As was the case with Jesus's temptation in the wilderness, Satan targets those relationships (to self, others, and God) for undermining and corruption. We may be particularly blessed in one of these areas, while subject to struggle in one or both of the others. To the extent we lack harmony among all three, we struggle to realize the fullness God meant for us. Calvin's nature

7. See a fuller discussion of this in Callaway, *Crossroads of the Eternal*, 94.
8. Chamblin, *Paul and the Self*, 31–33.

was a uniquely effective combination of these relationships. We are in such an awful condition today because we have for a long time tried to govern, educate, conduct our business, conduct our marriages, even worship in our churches without immersing our actions in the context of God's word and seeking honest, authentic feedback from it relative to these relationships. This was exactly the state of things when Calvin began his work in Geneva.

CALVIN'S FIRST STAY IN GENEVA

I already mentioned that the Genevans were very licentious. This was largely due to the influence of libertines who had grossly twisted the Reformation mantra of salvation by faith alone in Christ alone, to mean that they could live however they wanted. Their behavior was putting into practice the very things that Paul had been accused of advocating and stringently denied: "Are we to continue to sin that grace may abound?" (Rom 6:1). It was a clear example of a breakdown in the tri-perspectival relationships of self, others, and God. The breakdown always occurs with a distortion of the context provided by God's word, as Satan attempted to do in his temptation of Jesus. He even quoted Scripture to Jesus (Luke 4:10) but used it in a distorted context of putting God to the test. This is what the libertines in Geneva were doing, and is what we often do.

So how did Calvin and Farel go about addressing the situation? In short, they began a program of restoring discipline—both self-discipline and the kind of discipline in which citizens willingly uphold the law because of its protection of the rights and liberties of others. This was done by rightly and boldly teaching God's word and confronting misrepresentations of it. A famous example that came very early in Calvin's time in Geneva was at a disputation in Lausanne. Disputations—formal, public debates to move public opinion—were fairly common at that time. Switzerland was a confederation of semiautonomous states, or cantons. Some of the cantons had already decided to support the Reformation. The Canton of Vaud where Lausanne is located was still undecided, hence the disputation. Lausanne was a large city and its decision

Calvin's Personality and Initial Reception in Geneva

would influence the direction of other cantons in Switzerland. Farel wanted very much to go and asked Calvin to join him in the journey, which he did with no intention of participating in the disputation. Farel and Viret, another close friend of Calvin, were to represent the Reformation. They were both much older and more experienced than Calvin and were opposed by some very capable representatives from the Catholic Church. The disputation took place over an entire day and included debate of ten articles. As the debate progressed, Farel and Viret were struggling to make their case. Opinion was moving towards the Catholics, and a restlessness in the audience slowly grew to a murmur and began to become a clamor. Calvin, reserved and reluctant to speak, still a young man of only twenty-seven years, relatively unknown and new to his position, finally rose to speak. He had no notes and spoke only from memory. He exhibited such a broad and deep mastery of the Bible and the church fathers that he continued to speak for about an hour. He quoted very accurately long passages from the writings of Chrysostom, Cyprian, and others, noting precisely where the quotes came from in their works. As he continued to speak the clamor of the audience turned to a hushed awe and finally opinion was completely turned to the Reformers. After Calvin sat down, prominent Franciscan monk John Tandy is quoted as saying, "Based on what I have just heard, I confess that I have sinned against the Spirit and rebelled against the truth. Because of ignorance I have lived in error and spread wrong teaching. I ask God's pardon and the forgiveness of the people of Lausanne. I give up my role as friar; from now on I will follow Christ and his pure teaching alone."[9]

THE POWER OF GOD'S WORD TO CHANGE HEARTS

What an amazing example of Calvin's God-given abilities! It was an early indication of what lay ahead for him. But more importantly it was an example of the power of God's word working to

---

9. Hannula, *Trial and Triumph*, 133; Gore, "23. Life and Times," 32:10.

change the hearts of men. It is a tremendous testimony to Friar Tandy, too, to his humility and sincerity to seek honest feedback from God's word as applied to his life. God has many, many Friar Tandys out there. They are living in ignorance, doing what they sincerely believe to be right, and yet are lost. It took a lot to get Calvin to stand up and speak. The debate was almost lost. It would have been so easy for him to have remained seated. It would have been much more comfortable. He could have avoided the fear of saying the wrong thing, or being confronted by someone of great influence or better speaking ability. He must have felt the tug of God's hand lifting him up out of his seat. None of us is John Calvin. God equipped and used him in a very special way. But then neither was Calvin you or me. God has equipped each of us in a very special, but different way. Calvin was used to move mountains. God may have chosen us to move grains of sand, or much bigger things. We just don't know until we take his hand, rise up out of our chair, and speak. Very often by consistently standing up against the little things that may seem too absurd to bother contesting, God uses you to protect much bigger things. Ayn Rand observed, "The uncontested absurdities of today are the accepted slogans of tomorrow. They come to be accepted by degrees, by dint of constant pressure on one side and constant retreat on the other—until one day when they are suddenly declared to be the country's official ideology."[10] We see this happening all around us today, and we have a duty to be stewards and protectors of the truth.

Duty is a word we do not hear much anymore. It is a word Calvin knew well. It is a word that all true Calvinists know well because it's an obligation that God has placed upon the heart of each one of us. I am sure Calvin finally rose out of a feeling of duty to defend God's truth. In spiritual war, the same as any other, the battle must be engaged. Battles can never be won that are avoided at all costs. We have been cowed, intimidated out of the arena. We have taken ourselves off of the battlefield, even when the battle comes within the walls of the church. In obedience to God and literally for the sake of all that is good—because all that is good comes from

---

10. Rand, *Return of the Primitive*, 8.

Calvin's Personality and Initial Reception in Geneva

God—we *must* get back on the battlefield! Where is the sacrificial offering of ourselves—our egos, our status, our resources, our lives? "For whoever would save his life will lose it, but whoever loses his life for my sake will find it," Jesus said (Matt 16:25). In a similar vein historian A. J. Froude points out: "If we think of religion only as a means of escaping the wrath to come, we won't escape it because we're already under it. We are under the burden of death, for we care only for ourselves. This was not the religion of your fathers; this was not the Calvinism which overthrew spiritual wickedness, and hurled kings from their thrones, and purged England and Scotland, for a time at least, of lies and charlatanry."[11]

APPLICATION: TODAY'S DEARTH OF CALVINISM

A recent issue of *Decision* magazine had an article entitled "What's Wrong with America's Pulpits?"[12] A few of the statistics about pastors given in the article from a study conducted by George Barna are the following: Only one in three pastors surveyed (37 percent) had a biblical worldview and interpret the world through the lens of Scripture. The same percentage said that having faith matters more than which faith you have. Thirty-nine percent of evangelical pastors rejected that there is absolute moral truth. Instead, they believed that each individual must determine their own truth. It has been said, "Calvinism [is] the spirit which rises in revolt against untruth."[13] When only 61 percent of pastors believe there is absolute moral truth, we have already strayed far from our Calvinistic heritage. Only 62 percent of pastors agreed that human life is sacred. These and other sad measures of the faith of our pastors indicate how many of our spiritual "generals" have no interest in engaging the enemy. In fact, they recognize neither an enemy nor a battle. I'm reminded of what Sun Tzu says in *The Art of War*: "To fight and conquer in all your battles is not supreme excellence;

11. McFetridge, *Calvinism in History*, 17.
12. Weeks, "What's Wrong."
13. McFetridge, *Calvinism in History*, 17.

supreme excellence consists in breaking down the enemy's resistance without fighting."[14] This is what has happened in an appalling number of even our evangelical churches. The result is that today, based on Barna's seven cornerstones of a biblical worldview, only 6 percent of American adults actually have a biblical worldview.[15] When one third of all pastors do not read the Bible in a typical week, is it any wonder that the defense of biblical truth is so lacking?

In chapter 2 we quoted Scripture from Acts, in which Peter and the apostles were brought before the religious leaders of their day and strictly charged to stop teaching in the name of Jesus. Their reply was "We must obey God rather than men." How can we obey God rather than men when we ignore what God has revealed to us in his word? When so many of our shepherds do not even bother to read the Bible, is it any wonder the sheep are lost and devoured by wolves? This is a dereliction of duty and a sin against the body of Christ. But Christ did not abandon us to this. He has adopted us as his children and remains faithful. As the remnant of the faithful in Geneva were used under the right preaching of God's word by Calvin and Farel to transform a lost and licentious city, we, too, can be so used. May we pray for that grace.

---

14. Tzu, *Art of War*, 34.
15. Weeks, "What's Wrong," para. 15. The seven cornerstones include (para. 23):
   1. God is the eternal, omnipotent, omniscient, and just Creator.
   2. Humans are sinful by nature.
   3. Jesus Christ grants forgiveness of sin and eternal life when sinners repent and profess their faith in him alone.
   4. The Bible is true, reliable, and always relevant.
   5. Absolute moral truth exists.
   6. Success is defined as consistent obedience to God.
   7. Life's purpose is to know, love, and serve God with all one's heart, mind, strength, and soul.

STUDY QUESTIONS

1. Which three personality traits were particularly notable in Calvin?
2. Which three relationships are necessary for us to reflect as God's image bearers?
3. Why is it important to uphold God's truth even on things that might seem smaller concerns?

5

Calvinism as a Force

> Give the king your justice, O God, and your righteousness to the royal son! May he judge your people with righteousness, and your poor with justice! May he have dominion from sea to sea, and from the River to the ends of the earth! . . . May all kings fall down before him, all nations serve him! . . . May his name endure forever, his fame continue as long as the sun! May people be blessed in him, all nations call him blessed! Blessed be the Lord, the God of Israel, who alone does wondrous things. Blessed be his glorious name forever; may the whole earth be filled with his glory! Amen and Amen!
>
> —Ps 72:1–2, 8, 11, 17–19

BEFORE WE LAUNCH INTO the spread of Calvinism from Geneva to England, Scotland, and America, I want to leap ahead and look backwards. Specifically, with the clarity of hindsight I want to show why Calvinism has had such influence and has spread across the world. To do so we need to think of Calvinism as the force that

Calvinism as a Force

it is. As we saw in earlier chapters, it is a power to the extent that it is faithful to God and his word. It finds its power from God's power. It is only through God's power that rulers exercise dominion over their nations. And when rulers seek to please God, their peoples and nations are blessed. In a representative government like America's, we the people rule. When we neglect that duty, that obedience to God, God withdraws his blessings. Our founders understood this. To celebrate the victory of the Revolutionary War, Massachusetts governor John Hancock issued a proclamation for a Day of Thanksgiving on December 11, 1783. The day was to be spent "religiously . . . offering up fervent supplications . . . to cause pure religion and virtue to flourish . . . and to fill the world with his glory."[1] It could easily have found its inspiration from Ps 72:19. Filling the world with God's glory has been a recurring theme wherever Calvinism has been sincerely practiced. In this chapter, we will consider how it has served as a channel of God's power to the nations of the world.

We are at the point in our story where Calvin begins to influence much more than what goes on inside the walls of churches or seminaries. What will eventually be known as "Calvinism" is about to be launched upon the city of Geneva. Little did anyone, including Calvin, realize at that moment that a force was being unleashed, the impact of which has been so immensely transformative and enduring that it cannot be concisely summarized. It began by changing the city of Geneva from a licentious, squabbling, all-too-ordinary European town to a crown jewel. From there it spread to raise England to its greatest heights, to turn Scotland from a backwards, struggling country to one in which books are written about how the Scots invented the modern world.[2] From there it crossed the Atlantic and raised a nation up out of wilderness to be the world's greatest superpower. But more importantly, and in fact resulting from its uncompromising commitment to God through faith in Jesus Christ as a personal Savior, the fruit of Calvinism came forth.

1. Lee, *American Patriot Bible*, 648.
2. Herman, *How the Scots Invented*.

Calvinism and the Emergence of the Modern World

There is a great little book called *Calvinism in History*, by Nathaniel S. McFetridge, which has just four chapters. Each chapter covers Calvinism as a force in the world. Chapter 1 is Calvinism as a political force. Chapter 2 is its political force specific to America, which we will cover in a later chapter of the present book. Chapter 3 is Calvinism as a moral force. And chapter 4 is Calvinism as an evangelizing force, which we covered in our previous chapter. In this chapter we will cover Calvinism's moral and political forces.

CALVINISM AS A MORAL FORCE

In attempting to describe the most impactful characteristics of Calvinism, I listed a sense of duty as arguably most important. Duty and conscience are closely linked. Doing your duty is putting what weighs on your conscience into action, as in "Here I am, Lord" (Gen 22:1). McFetridge says, "If there is one characteristic of Calvinistic morality more prominent than another, it is conscience."[3] Founding Father and our sixth president John Quincy Adams called the colony of New England "a colony of conscience."[4] McFetridge makes a very compelling argument as to why this matters. There are two fundamental ways by which we are moved, and thereby shaped for better or worse. They are by sentiment and by conviction. Another way to phrase it is to say by emotion or ideas. Emotions rise and fall with changing circumstances. They are affected by what we see, hear, smell, or taste. They place us at the mercy of externals—things that happen to us. On the other hand, convictions are stable. If someone has the conviction that we are sinners before an Almighty God, that God's laws are true, unchanging, and good, and that we cannot save ourselves from our sinful state, then those convictions turn one away from the pursuit of useless, fluctuating things of man and created things and towards God the Creator and Ruler of all things. Their conviction that God and the things of God are what truly matter leads to

---

3. McFetridge, *Calvinism in History*, 75.
4. McFetridge, *Calvinism in History*, 75.

Calvinism as a Force

a deep sense of duty. This overriding conviction of how the world works, which we call "worldview," is what sets Calvinists apart. A sense of duty runs deep in every true Calvinist. The fact that duty is a word that is rarely heard today—and when it is heard it is often mischaracterized as a kind of blind stubbornness—shows how far we have drifted from our Calvinist heritage. People with a deep sense of duty to a good, true, holy, and just God are people who are constantly evaluating themselves to identify where they are lacking and making changes in their life. Their consciences spur them to a greater and greater purity of mind, heart, and action. They never "rest on their laurels." But because they also have a deep conviction of God's love for his children, the stereotype of being gloomy Christians is inaccurate.

A second characteristic of a true Calvinist that is almost a by-product of conviction is courage. This is due to the stability of convictions as compared with someone who is moved by emotions. If a reality is stable, one who holds to that reality must stand firm. Standing firm requires courage. The plague of wokeness that we see today is very powerful, but it is a plague that is "a mile wide and an inch deep." It is very fragile. If its strength in numbers erodes beyond a certain point, it will crumble quickly. It is truly a house built on sand, although right now there is an awful lot of sand. McFetridge summarizes how conscience and courage go together: "Men of conscience are, other things being equal, the brave men, the bold men, the courageous men. Calvinism, by appealing to conscience and emphasizing duty, begets a moral heroism which has been the theme of song and praise for centuries."[5] The great historian (and not a Calvinist) George Bancroft quipped, "A coward and a Puritan never went together."[6]

---

5. McFetridge, *Calvinism in History*, 78.
6. McFetridge, *Calvinism in History*, 80.

Calvinism and the Emergence of the Modern World

FRUITS OF CALVINISM AS A MORAL FORCE

So what are some of the fruits of Calvinism as a moral force? There are many! I'd like to share a few quotes from various people, most not being Calvinists themselves. James Anthony Froude had this to say when giving an address to the church of St. Andrew's in March of 1871: "I am going to ask you to consider how it came to pass that if Calvinism is indeed the hard and unreasonable creed which modern enlightenment declares it to be, it has possessed such singular attractions in past times for some of the greatest men that ever lived . . . why, if it be a creed of intellectual servitude, it was able to inspire and sustain the bravest efforts ever made by man to break the yoke of unjust authority?"[7] A historian and critic of Calvin had this to say about Calvinism's positive impact on the world: "Grave as we may count the faults of Calvinism, alien as its temper may in many ways be from the temper of the modern world, it is in Calvinism that the modern world strikes its roots; for it was Calvinism that first revealed the worth and dignity of man. Called of God and heir of heaven, the trader at his counter and the digger in his field suddenly rose into equality with the noble and the king." He went further to say, "Home, as we conceive it, was the creation of the Puritans."[8] McFetridge claims that in all the history of Puritanism there is not a single example of a divorce. With regard to honesty, Froude says, "The Calvinists were the men who abhorred, as no body of men ever more abhorred, all conscious mendacity, all impurity, all moral wrong of every kind so far as they could recognize it. Whatever exists at this moment in England and Scotland of conscientious fear of doing evil is the remnant of the convictions which were branded by the Calvinists into people's hearts."[9] This reputation for honesty is commented on by Henry Ward Beecher: "Men may talk as much as they please against the Calvinists and Puritans and Presbyterians, but you will find that when they want to make an investment they have

---

7. McFetridge, *Calvinism in History*, 81.
8. McFetridge, *Calvinism in History*, 84.
9. McFetridge, *Calvinism in History*, 85.

Calvinism as a Force

no objection to Calvinism or Puritanism or Presbyterianism. They know that where these systems prevail, where the doctrine of men's obligations to God and man is taught and practiced, there their capital may be safely invested."[10] Calvinism has had very favorable influence on reducing crime too. McFetridge observes, "That is certainly a remarkable coincidence, that where there is the most of Calvinism there is the least of crime."[11] And Froude again remarks, "The Calvinists have been called intolerant; but intolerance of an enemy who is trying to kill you seems to me a pardonable state of mind."[12] It seems to me that we could use a lot more of this common sense today.

And speaking of common sense, should we really be spending as much time as we do entertaining ourselves? Should our youth find nothing more compelling and important than playing games and watching videos on their phone? The Calvinist would emphatically say no! "Life to them," McFetridge says of Calvinists, "was an experience too noble and earnest and solemn to be frittered away . . . They felt, in the innermost core of their hearts, that life was short and its responsibilities great. Hence their religion was their life."[13]

One does not have to be old to have witnessed a drift away from religion that in the last very few years has turned into a stampede. Has that led to more or less peace, more or less caring for others, more or less crime, better or poorer financial situations? We have neglected our responsibilities, and time is indeed short to avoid severe and lasting consequences for doing so.

CALVINISM AS A POLITICAL FORCE

We just saw some of the ways Calvinism has been a transformational positive force for morality in our world. What about for

10. McFetridge, *Calvinism in History*, 86.
11. McFetridge, *Calvinism in History*, 89.
12. McFetridge, *Calvinism in History*, 90.
13. McFetridge, *Calvinism in History*, 91.

politics? Has it had similar benefits in that sphere in which we establish our priorities as a society or nation, where we agree on the framework of behaviors and boundaries, the norms through which we interact with others, and work out our differences without the use of coercive force?

As mentioned, how we think about God determines how we view ourselves and others. Our worldview influences our conduct and our character. Froude says, "As long as we look upon God as an exactor, not a giver, exactors, not givers, we shall be."[14] A. A. Hodge argues that there are only three fundamental systems of doctrine:

1. That which "denies the guilt, corruption and moral impotence of man, and makes him independent of the supernatural assistance of God." This is called Pelagianism.

2. At the opposite end of the spectrum, Calvinism "emphasizes the guilt and moral impotence of man, exalts the justice and sovereignty of God, and refers salvation absolutely to the undeserved favor and new creative energy of God."

3. In between these two is a kind of compromise position called "Arminianism," or sometimes "semi-Pelagianism," which "admits man's original corruption, but denies his guilt; regards redemption as a compensation for innate, and consequently irresponsible, disabilities; and refers the moral restoration of the individual to the co-operation of the human with the divine energy, the determining factor being the human will."[15]

Going forward I will consider Pelagianism and Arminianism as a single form of doctrine and call them "Arminianism" versus Calvinism. Arminianism and Calvinism have two different forms of worship. And that is not coincidental, but inherent. McFetridge makes this important summary of which we will follow the implications: "A system of doctrine, as Pelagianism, which teaches salvation by our own good works or, as Arminianism, which teaches salvation partly by works and partly by grace, of necessity

---

14. McFetridge, *Calvinism in History*, 2.
15. McFetridge, *Calvinism in History*, 4.

sympathizes and affiliates with rites and ceremonies, and lays, in the very spirit of it, the foundation for a ritualistic service."[16] Then he quotes a historian named Buckle, saying, "It is an interesting fact that the doctrines which in England are called Calvinistic have always been connected with a democratic spirit, while those of Arminianism have found most favor among the aristocratic."[17] As worship follows doctrine, so civil government follows both. "Thus we see how Arminianism, taking to an aristocratic form of church government, tends toward a monarchy in civil affairs, while Calvinism, taking to a republican form of church government, tends toward a democracy in civil affairs."[18] Monarchs have understood this well. Charles of England said, "No bishop, no king." By this he meant that if there is no despotic power in the church, there could be no despotic power in the state. Unlike Lutheranism, Calvinism never had the almost submissive relationship with princes. In his book *Presbyterians and the Revolution*, W. P. Breed says, "Calvinism is in fact a system of government—a method and form in which the divine power is put forth in the administration of the affairs of the universe. It is based on the idea that God rules; that he has a plan; that the plan is fixed and certain; that is does not depend on the human will. . . . It supposes that God is supreme; that he has authority; that he has a right to exercise dominion."[19]

DESPOTISM AND CHURCH POLITY

Another reason for Calvinism's hostility to despotism and positive influence for civil liberty is its church polity. The clergy and clergymen participate equally in the official acts of the church. The same is expected from civil government. Yet another reason for the salutary effect of Calvinism on liberty is its theology. It upholds the

16. McFetridge, *Calvinism in History*, 6.
17. McFetridge, *Calvinism in History*, 6–7.
18. McFetridge, *Calvinism in History*, 7.
19. Breed, *Presbyterians and the Revolution*, 19–20. See also Bulkeley, *Hope for the Children*, for an excellent discussion of how man-centered worship is popularized in modern American churches, along with the consequences.

fact that we have an almighty God who rules all of creation and every minute detail of it. He does not let a sparrow fall without his knowledge and numbers every hair on our heads. How can anyone who truly believes this submit to the dictates of a tyrant who makes demands in opposition to God? It has been rightly noted, "Laws express the will of a sovereign lord of a social order, and, as such, they express the working religion of the state and its people. If the state or the people have differing religions, there will be conflict between the two, because each then has a different concept of government. Government like law is a theological concept; it is revelatory of the god of a system or a society. Among other things, God is government, as well as love, justice, mercy, redemption, and more. There can be no salvation if God is not also the absolute government over all things. How else can God redeem us if He does not absolutely govern all things?"[20] Ultimately, the government indeed rests upon God's shoulders (Is 9:6). This is anathema to all other forms of government in which man sits in the place of God either in the form of kings, the state, or the priesthood.

While the conflict is to acknowledge who is sovereign—God or men—the battle is fought for the hearts, minds, and souls of individuals. Marxists say, "If socialism is against human nature, then human nature must be changed."[21] Of course human nature cannot be changed without causing man to cease to be man. Marxists and similar ideologues are those described by C. S. Lewis in *The Abolition of Man*: "They have sacrificed their own share in traditional humanity in order to devote themselves to the task of deciding what 'humanity' shall henceforth mean."[22] Man was created by God in God's image. Nevertheless, defining what humanity shall henceforth mean is the objective of those standing in opposition to God's sovereignty. "Totalitarianism is much more than mere bureaucracy. It is the subordination of every individual's whole life, work, and leisure, to the orders of those in power and office.... It forces the individual to renounce any activity of which

---

20. Rushdoony, *Sovereignty*, 8.
21. Rushdoony, *Sovereignty*, 9.
22. Lewis, *Abolition of Man*, 63.

the government does not approve. It tolerates no expression of dissent. It is a transformation of society."[23] Do the lockdowns and mandates that were forced upon the world during the COVID-19 pandemic make more sense now? They were never a rational, science-based response to the spread of a virus so much as they were a statement from leaders in government about who is in control.

THE CALVINIST

Calvinism and its doctrine of freedom from slavery to the false sovereignty of men as we realize and accept our adoption as children of God in Christ is a direct threat to man's claim of sovereignty. Rather than being beholden to the dictates of the state or other forms of hierarchy, "every man in Christ," says Rushdoony, "must be a walking law and an evidence of the presence of the Holy Spirit. God's government of the world begins with the self-government of the Christian man."[24] In the same way Calvinism is an affront to hierarchies among men. Its doctrine affirms an equality of men before a holy God.

Even among more common acquaintances this conviction about who God is and how he rules tends to "level the field." Men may certainly differ in their God-given gifts, but before the Almighty "all of our righteous deeds are but filthy rags" (Isa 64:6). Our righteousness is from God as determined by his electing grace. This doctrine of predestination for which Calvinism is well known is despised by all with a despotic tendency. Why? Again, McFetridge sums it up beautifully:

> This doctrine inspires a resolute, almost defiant, freedom in those who deem themselves the subjects of God's electing grace; in all things they are more than conquerors through the confidence that nothing shall be able to separate them from the love of God. No doctrine of the dignity of human nature, of the rights of man, of natural liberty, of social equality, can create such a resolve for

23. Rushdoony, *Sovereignty*, 9.
24. Rushdoony, *Sovereignty*, 11.

the freedom of the soul as this personal conviction of God's favoring and protecting sovereignty. He who has this faith feels that he is compassed about with everlasting love, guided with everlasting strength; his will is the tempered steel that no fire can melt, no force can break. Such faith is freedom; and this spiritual freedom is the source and strength of all other freedom.[25]

What a wonderful explanation of the practical outworking of Calvinism in political society!

In our subsequent chapters we will look at some of the consequences of the doctrines of Calvinism as we follow their application across geographies, nations, and time. As others have put it, "Christ is the key to the history of the world. The spiritual will always body itself forth in the temporal history of man."[26] As the descendants and beneficiaries of the legacy of Calvinism in service of Christ and his glory, we have a special duty to carry the standard forward; teach the actual world-changing manifestations to the glory of God; and model through our humility, boldness, and firmness of faith the power of God in even his weakest vessels to the younger generations. We pray that he might find us faithful.

STUDY QUESTIONS

1. What are the two fundamental ways humans are moved to action?
2. How do duty and courage interact as a moral force in society? How has this been a force of Calvinism?
3. What are the three basic systems of doctrine described by A. A. Hodge?
4. How do Arminianism and Calvinism differ in their worship styles and, indirectly, concepts of government?
5. Why is Calvinism a direct threat to tyranny?

25. McFetridge, *Calvinism in History*, 13.
26. McFetridge, *Calvinism in History*, 13.

6

Calvin's Wandering Years and Return to Geneva

> "Behold, the king is sitting at the gate." And all the people came before the king. Now Israel had fled every man to his own home. And all the people were arguing throughout all the tribes of Israel, saying, "The king delivered us from the hand of our enemies and saved us from the hand of the Philistines, and now he has fled out of the land from Absalom. But Absalom, whom we anointed over us, is dead in battle. Now therefore why do you say nothing about bringing the king back?"
>
> —2 Sam 19:8b–10

JOHN CALVIN AND THE city of Geneva share an intertwined history. There was a time when Geneva could have been called "the city of Calvin," as Jerusalem is "the city of David." But before that association of Calvin and Geneva, there was, like David from Jerusalem, a period of exile followed by reinstatement. That will be part of the story we cover here.

Calvinism and the Emergence of the Modern World

In earlier chapters we spoke of Calvin's entry into Geneva for the first time. And, we spent some time discussing certain characteristics of the man as well as those of the doctrinal system of Calvinism in terms of why it has been such a transformational force for civilization. We also spoke of why there is such an urgent need to return to an application of those doctrines in our lives and society, starting in our homes and churches. Now we will continue with his time in Geneva and the years immediately following.

CALVIN'S FIRST STAY IN GENEVA

To address the licentious behavior of the populace, Calvin and Farel began a program of discipline and education. They developed a Confession of Faith and Discipline and Calvin produced a popular catechism. Both of these were approved by the Genevan city council in 1536. The confession was a precursor to confessions we are familiar with today, such as the Belgic and Helvetic Confessions. The catechism was widely used beyond Geneva, was translated into several languages, and provided much of the material for the Heidelberg Catechism and Westminster Confession. By 1537 people were coming from far and wide to see what was happening in Geneva and the two men behind it. In July of that same year the ruling Council of Two Hundred ordered that all citizens assent to the confession. Any who did not would be banished. The fact that these people who had just escaped from the yoke of the pope were now being subjected to a human creed was not received well at all. This, which neither Calvin nor Farel was responsible for ordering, along with the discipline, including excommunication, which they clearly were responsible for implementing, led to their expulsion from Geneva. Things had come to a head during Easter of 1538 and there was an air of violence. In April of 1538, both Farel and Calvin were deposed without trial and given three days to leave town. They eventually admitted they had been too rigid, but by then they were already exiled. The two were warmly received in Basel, Switzerland, but did not stay there long. Farel accepted a call to Neuchâtel, and Calvin left two months later to

Calvin's Wandering Years and Return to Geneva

go to Strasbourg at the invitation of Martin Bucer, arriving there in September of 1538. He spent three lean but productive years as pastor and professor. It was during this time that he became close friends with Philip Melanchthon, German Reformer and associate of Martin Luther.

TIME OF EXILE

In 1539 a very eloquent and powerful Catholic cardinal named Sadolet attempted to reclaim Geneva for the pope. He had been one of the secretaries of the very corrupt Pope Leo X and was frequently asked to serve in diplomatic negotiations between the king of France and the emperor of Germany. His opening salvo in the battle to reclaim the church at Geneva was through a flattering, seductive letter to the city leaders. It was followed by a group of citizens protesting the ordinance by which the Confession of Faith had been adopted. City leaders were facing a serious emerging threat from Rome, but had no one capable of answering it. Calvin had been sent a copy of Sadolet's letter and, though he had not been mentioned by name, the Reformation was clearly under attack. He felt it his duty to reply, and he did. He masterfully countered and destroyed each point made by Sadolet. In his old age now, Martin Luther had received a copy of Calvin's response to Sadolet and was very pleased. He told a friend, "This answer has hand and foot, and I rejoice that God raises up men who will give the last blow to popery, and finish the war against Antichrist which I began."[1] Calvin's letter also made a lasting impression on the Geneva City Council and saved them from the conniving attack by Rome.

But the most important event for Calvin during this time was his marriage to Idelette Stordeur de Bure in August of 1540. We saw in chapter 4 how happy he was with her and how she tragically died a mere nine years later. Calvin would survive her by fifteen years.

Meanwhile, back in Geneva things had deteriorated since the expulsion of Calvin and Farel. Three competing parties had

---

1. Schaff, *Modern Christianity*, 412.

formed. One has been referred to as the government party, and was hostile to the Reformers. It was protected by Bern because members of this party had secretly negotiated and signed a treaty with Bern conceding to them their sovereignty. They also supported subjection of the church to the state. These actions were considered treasonous by much of the population. Within two years after Calvin and Farel had been banished, the four leaders who had caused their banishment all came to unfortunate ends. One was beheaded for homicide and sedition. Two others were condemned to death as forgers and rebels. And the fourth died from a wound he received while attempting to escape justice. With these turns of events, this anti-reform party was soon dead. The second party was the Roman Catholics. Calvin's letter to Sadolet devastated their ambitions to return to power. The third party was friendly to the Reformers. They had maintained correspondence with Calvin and Farel and had been working to encourage them to return. Now they felt the time was right to recall them to Geneva.

It is fair to say that Calvin's first stint in Geneva was not one of which he had a lot of fond memories. It is also clear that he had comfortably settled in to Strasbourg. His Sunday services were crowded. His theological lectures drew students from several countries. He was happily married and finally able to enjoy domestic life. He was even appreciated by the government. And he enjoyed the company of the likes of Bucer and Melanchthon. When considering a return to Geneva, he confided to his friend Viret, "There is no place in the world which I fear more; not because I hate it, but because I feel unequal to the difficulties which await me there."[2] Why would he do such a thing as return? He answers that question in a letter to Farel. "When I remember," he said, "that in this matter I am not my own master, I present my heart as a sacrifice and offer it up to the Lord."[3] What a beautifully selfless, sacrificial heart! And how characteristic! As I have immersed myself in studying Calvin and the influence of Calvinism in doing so much good in both this life and in preparation

2. Schaff, *Modern Christianity*, 429.
3. Schaff, *Modern Christianity*, 429.

for the life to come, and in seeing that beneficial influence face down the mightiest empires and raise up even mightier nations, I have looked to find a concise way to sum up how it happens. Of course it is the hand of God at work through his people. But I have searched for the best way to describe how the Holy Spirit manifests this power in his people. I haven't found a better statement than Calvin's to Farel: "In this matter I am not my own master, I present my heart as a sacrifice and offer it up to the Lord." Whether it is the young soldier storming a machine-gun nest in Nazi Germany, a whistleblower bringing forward evidence of corruption in the FBI, or a parent standing up to a school board that is complicit in the rape of his daughter due to their CRT policies,[4] we hear echoes of those words. "In this matter I am not my own master, I present my heart as a sacrifice and offer it up to the Lord." Our faith is like a breaker to a power line carrying electricity into our home. At any point in our lives when we forget that we are not our own master, we throw the breaker and lose our connection to the source of power. When we are in the heat of an argument and winning the argument becomes more important than offering our heart through it to God, we throw that breaker. When we agree with the words or behaviors of others who are sinning against God and "go along to get along," we throw that breaker. Our sins of omission are often more damaging than are our sins of commission because we tell ourselves, "When I saw him do that, I refused to help him in his sinning. I didn't encourage him." Well, what did you do to help him see his sin and turn his heart? Especially in today's woke world of "safe spaces" and "words are violence," the whole point of wokeness is to intimidate others into committing sins of omission, not saying anything when we see evil. For the sake of our own souls and for the souls of those around us we need to recover our Calvinistic heritage and live in the knowledge that "in this matter I am not my own master, I present my heart as a sacrifice and offer it up to the Lord," and then act!

---

4. CRT stands for critical race theory, a divisive theory that is in itself racist, which originated from the work of German Marxist academics.

Calvin was not misguided in his trepidation of returning to Geneva. Years later he looked back on those years of his second stint there and said, "Although the welfare of that Church was so dear to me that I could without difficulty sacrifice my life for it; yet my timidity presented to me many reasons of excuse for declining to take such a heavy burden on my shoulders. But the sense of duty prevailed and led me to return to the flock from which I had been snatched away. I did this with sadness, tears, and great anxiety and distress of mind, the Lord being my witness, and many pious persons who would gladly have spared me that pain, if not the same fear had shut their mouth."[5] Notice that he points out favorably those who didn't merely tell him what he wanted to hear. They were being loving shepherds to him by telling him what they believed God wanted him to hear. And at least in the case of Martin Bucer, he also stood to lose the personal benefit of Calvin working with him for the continued good of Strasbourg. Recognizing this, Calvin specifically mentions Bucer and calls him "that excellent servant of Christ."[6] You see, Bucer had reminded Calvin of Jonah's example: he reminded him to be obedient to God's call on his life.

CALVIN'S RETURN

So without going into the negotiations between the delegation from Geneva, those who wanted him to stay in Strasbourg, and his own conflicting emotions and consideration of his friends and family, we will continue with the knowledge that Calvin did in fact return to Geneva. He arrived back in Geneva in September of 1541, just over three years after he had been exiled. He remained there until his death twenty-three years later on May 27, 1564, working prolifically. The work ethic of Calvinists is axiomatic, and Calvin embodied it. He well understood the mystery of God's sovereignty and man's call to action and work. He pointed out, "God, after freely bestowing his grace on us, forthwith demands of us

---

5. Schaff, *Modern Christianity*, 430.
6. Schaff, *Modern Christianity*, 430.

Calvin's Wandering Years and Return to Geneva

a reciprocal acknowledgment. When he said to Abraham, 'I am thy God,' it was an offer of his free goodness; but he adds at the same time what he required of him: 'Walk before me, and be thou perfect.' This condition is tacitly annexed to all the promises. They are to be to us as spurs, inciting us to promote the glory of God."[7]

Meanwhile, God was setting the stage for the next acts in his eternal plan. In England, Scotland, and elsewhere, as we will see in upcoming chapters, players were coming upon the scene—Henry VIII (and his children), John Wycliff, John Knox, and others—who would directly or indirectly be confronted with the teachings emanating from this little man in the modest city of Geneva.

But before we leave this place and time and move to England in our next chapter, there are a couple of subjects that need to be dealt with. The first is the myth of "the dictator of Geneva." And the second, related, is what is often called "the Servetus affair."

"THE DICTATOR OF GENEVA"

Alister McGrath, in his biography of Calvin, suggests that like all lasting myths, there is an element of truth in this myth that Calvin ruled Geneva as a dictator during his second stint there. To keep us from bogging down in the minutiae of this topic, which is really not a primary focus of this book, let me simply say that the element of truth is that Calvin did attempt to institute "theocratic rule" in Geneva. However, what is meant by this and what is usually implied are two quite different things. McGrath probably comes closest in describing what Calvin was trying to accomplish, which was "a regime in which all authority is recognized to derive from God."[8] What has been implied for centuries, thus creating the myth, is that Calvin implemented oppressive religious laws to force strict adherence to them and punished any deviation from them with dictatorial brutality in a kind of reign of terror. This myth is used to discredit Calvin and Calvinism, which are actually direct threats to

---

7. Schaff, *Modern Christianity*, 437–38.
8. McGrath, *Life of John Calvin*, 106.

tyranny and dictators. An example of the myth from fairly recent times is given in McGrath's biography of Calvin: Aldous Huxley asserted, without any evidence, "During the great Calvin's theocratic rule of Geneva a child was publicly decapitated for having ventured to strike its parents."[9] McGrath is able to quickly and easily refute this accusation. There is no record of any such incident in the Genevan archives, which are quite comprehensive. Second, there was no basis in the Genevan criminal or civil codes for such a punishment. But, if there had been, the laws were made by the city, not by Calvin. In fact, as a foreigner, Calvin could neither vote nor stand for office. He had no civil authority at all. What authority he had was moral authority through persuasion.

The unfairness of this myth is made more grotesque when Calvin's letters to his friends and his actual behavior are considered. When Calvin returned to Geneva, he was in a very strong position to seek revenge against his former opponents, or at least to remind them of what was clearly his victory over their persecution of him. However, he took great pains to do just the opposite. In a 1542 letter to a friend in Basel less than a year after his return to Geneva, Calvin wrote, "I value the public peace and concord so highly, that I lay restraint upon myself; and this praise even the adversaries are compelled to award to me. This feeling prevails to such an extent, that from day to day, those who were once open enemies have become friends; others I conciliate by courtesy, and I feel that I have been in some measure successful." He says this being fully aware that he had plenty of political capital to have been vindictive. "On my arrival it was in my power to have disconcerted our enemies most triumphantly, entering with full sail among the whole of that tribe who had done the mischief. I have abstained; if I had liked, I could daily, not merely with impunity, but with the approval of very many, have used sharp reproof. I forbear: even with the most scrupulous care do I avoid everything of the kind."[10]

Neither was Calvin a dictator outside of the political arena. Soon after he returned, a plague that had devastated surrounding

9. McGrath, *Life of John Calvin*, 105.
10. Schaff, *Modern Christianity*, 439.

Calvin's Wandering Years and Return to Geneva

nations reached Geneva. It decimated Geneva, killing a tenth of the entire population. Calvin offered to work in the houses of the sick, but was restrained by the ministers of the city. They would not allow him to leave his duties at the church or to expose himself to the plague.

THE SERVETUS AFFAIR

I am very reluctant to spend any time on this, but like the dictator of Geneva myth, it has been a persistent slander of Calvin and by association, Calvinists. McGrath says, "The trial and execution of Michael Servetus as a heretic have, more than any other event, colored Calvin's posthumous reputation."[11] So I feel I have to address it, even if briefly and superficially.

Michael Servetus was a Spanish physician whose studies had made some significant contributions to medical science; where he had gotten into controversy was with his positions on the Trinity. He had been imprisoned in France by the Catholic Church for heresy, but had escaped and was passing through Geneva and was caught. Calvin brought forward a list of thirty-eight accusations against him. Punishment for crimes, particularly capital punishment, was something that the city leaders were adamant against relinquishing. They sought input on guilt or innocence from Calvin and from the various Protestant cantons of Switzerland. But they determined the punishment and used a horrible, yet common, punishment at the time of burning at the stake. Calvin actually argued for a less cruel punishment of beheading. Calvin has received the brunt of the criticism for this even though Servetus was spared from burning at the hands of the French Catholic Church instead of the city of Geneva only because he had escaped their prison. He had been condemned as a heretic by both Catholic and Protestant Churches.

So with this we conclude the life of Calvin and move to the next chapter of his legacy. We will focus more on the influence of Calvinism on nations and less on the man or his theology per se.

11. McGrath, *Life of John Calvin*, 115.

STUDY QUESTIONS

1. Which key events led to Calvin being asked to return to Geneva?
2. Do you think Calvin's statement "in this matter I am not my own master, I present my heart as a sacrifice and offer it up to the Lord" is a good summary of Calvinism? Why, or why not?
3. Why is the assertion that Calvin acted as a dictator in Geneva false?
4. What was "the Servetus affair" and why should Calvin not be blamed for the execution of Servetus?

7

The Rise of Puritanism in England

> Hezekiah received the letter from the hand of the messengers and read it; and Hezekiah went up to the house of the Lord and spread it before the Lord. And Hezekiah prayed before the Lord and said: "O Lord, the God of Israel, enthroned above the cherubim, you are the God, you alone, of all the kingdoms of the earth: you have made heaven and earth."
>
> —2 Kgs 19:14–15

LAST CHAPTER WE SAW how Calvin, like David, had been exiled from the city that became synonymous with his name. It was only when he returned from exile that God used him in such powerful ways that would continue to influence the world for over five hundred years. Though human rulers are the most powerful in earthly terms, God's plan is in no jeopardy from them. In fact, he uses them to advance his sovereign and eternal plan. In this chapter, we will see how God's plan was advanced via Calvinism through the rise and fall of kings and queens.

Calvinism and the Emergence of the Modern World

HENRY VIII (1509-47)

To understand the spread of the Reformation to England, and Calvinism in particular, we have to delve into some of the goings-on of the monarchy. We begin with the arranged marriage of Henry VII's son Arthur to Catherine of Aragon, a daughter of King Ferdinand and Queen Isabella of Spain. As with many such arrangements, it was to strengthen political ties between Spain and England to counter the hostile alliance of Scotland and France. They married when Catherine was just fifteen years old. Then Arthur promptly died just four months later. This created a problem. Spain and England wanted to retain the ties established by the marriage, not to mention England wanting to keep the substantial widow's dowry. The next in line to the English throne was Arthur's younger brother Henry, but canon law prohibited the marriage of a man to his brother's widow. What to do? Well, you contact the pope and get him to give you a papal dispensation, which they did. Even so, there was uncertainty as to whether the pope had the power to grant one. And that created uncertainty around the legality of the arrangement. After several years of marriage with no male heir produced, the monarchy began looking for solutions. The only surviving child of Henry and Catherine was a daughter, Princess Mary Tudor. Henry had also fathered a bastard son, whom he made duke of Richmond. Efforts were made to legitimize this son. But the pope refused to act, fearing it would anger Spain. It was also suggested that the duke of Richmond marry Mary Tudor. This was also shot down as being even more illegitimate. Henry finally settled on requesting that the original marriage between himself and Catherine be annulled by the pope. This was not uncommon. However, the pope was practically controlled by Catherine's nephew, Charles V of Germany (the Holy Roman Empire). Catherine asked Charles to save her from dishonor by preventing the pope from granting an annulment. Henry then turned to his religious advisor, Thomas Cranmer, who suggested he consult with the main Catholic universities. They all declared his marriage was not valid. At this point, I will skip over a lot of interesting but only tangentially related material about Henry's other wives and their children. Several will enter the stage of this story in future chapters. The critical point here is that there was a rupture in the long-standing relationship between the Crown and the Catholic Church. The consequences of this would continue to ebb and flow for many decades.

It is important to note that Henry VIII was not a Protestant. As a young man and not then first in line for the crown, he had been trained for a religious position of some kind. As part of his studies, he had written a treatise against Luther that was so well done as to cause Pope Leo X to give him the title of "defender of the faith." The papacy would later come to regret this title. It shows once again that God has a sense of humor. Although Henry VIII did receive excellent training in his religious studies, the program concentrated on canon law and spent little time on biblical studies. This was rather typical at that time and largely explained his blind spots regarding the Reformation. For example, at Cranmer's instigation the Bible was translated into English, and by royal decree was placed in every church in England where all could read it. Henry's limited understanding of the Bible was that it was just about love and peace. He failed to understand what a powerful weapon it was for reform. The net result was that the Reformation established a firm foundation during his reign without Henry actually intending to support it.

With the schism between the Crown and Rome complete, Henry became head of the Church of England and quickly voided his marriage to Catherine and regularized a secret marriage he had had with Anne Boleyn, who was already pregnant with what he hoped would be a son. It wasn't. Their daughter was Elizabeth. His patience with Anne for not producing a male heir quickly expired. So he falsely accused her of adultery and condemned her to death. He then married Jane Seymour, who finally gave him the male heir he had desired for so long. The boy's name was Edward. Jane died in childbirth. It is said that Henry was asked at the point in which both her life and her child's were in danger, which should be saved.

He replied, "If you cannot save both, at least let the child live, for other wives are easily found."[1]

EDWARD VI (1547–53)

After Henry's death in 1547 Edward came to the throne at age ten and reigned for only six years before he also died. During those six years the Reformation made some important strides. Perhaps the most significant was the publication of the Book of Common Prayer, written primarily by Cranmer. It marked the first time that the English people had a liturgy in their own language. Other reforms included the return of the communion cup to the laity, allowing members of the clergy to marry, and the removal of images from churches. John Knox, whom we will discuss in more detail in a later chapter, made a cameo appearance in England in 1552 and was almost immediately installed as Edward's court preacher.

MARY TUDOR (1553–58)

Following Edward's death in 1553, the crown went to his half-sister, Mary Tudor, the daughter of Catherine of Aragon. Mary was and had always been a Catholic. She was not about to change, due both to religious convictions and political necessity. It was due to the schism with the Roman Catholic Church and the voiding of her mother's marriage to Henry that she had become a bastard child. Without the authority of the Roman Catholic Church, her legitimacy as queen remained in question. She had support from her cousin, Charles V. And she strategically married her cousin Philip of Spain, who abandoned her after two years and returned to Spain. Once she felt she had sufficiently consolidated her power, she made her move. In late 1554 she returned England in obedience to the pope. She began undoing the reforms that took place under Henry and Edward. And she began her brutal persecutions by which she earned the name "Bloody Mary." She began, as

1. Lancelott, "Jane Seymour," para. 13.

tyrants always do, by clamping down on what they claim is "disinformation." Books by Luther, Tyndale, and many other Reformers were banned. Then the persecutions intensified. She burned about three hundred Protestants and jailed many others. In addition, many went into exile to places like Calvin's Geneva. The inspiring story of Thomas Cranmer's martyrdom came during these years. Cranmer had been imprisoned and forced to watch the burning of his friends Hugh Latimer and Dr. Nicholas Ridley. Mary wanted to force a written recantation of his Reformed beliefs, which he reluctantly gave. With that in hand, she decided to burn him anyway unless he made his recantation publicly. This he began by speaking of his sins and weaknesses. Then, his comments took an unexpected turn. He recanted his recantation, saying, "They were written contrary to the truth which I thought in my heart, and written for fear of death, to save my life if it might be. . . . And forasmuch as I have written many things contrary to what I believe in my heart, my hand shall first be punished; for if I may come to the fire it shall first be burned. As for the Pope, I refuse him, for Christ's enemy and antichrist, with all his false doctrine."[2] This he did, extending his hand down into the flame first. In the blood of the martyrs shed by Bloody Mary the seed of the Reformed Church continued to grow. Mercifully for the Protestants, Mary died in 1558.

ELIZABETH (1558-1603)

Mary's half-sister Elizabeth, born to Anne Boleyn, followed Mary to the throne. Charles V had urged Mary to have Elizabeth killed. But for whatever reason, she never did. Now her policies were about to be undone. Just as Mary needed the Catholic Church's ruling about her mother to be valid to ensure the legitimacy of her rule, Elizabeth needed it to be invalid for her to legitimately rule because she had been born to Anne while Catherine was still living. In contrast to Bloody Mary, Elizabeth attempted to be quite tolerant to a wide latitude of religious opinions, as long as neither

---

2. González, *Story of Christianity*, 2:78.

Catholics nor Protestants took an extreme position. An illustration of her approach was expressed in the new Book of Common Prayer as pertains to communion: "The body of our Lord Jesus Christ which was given for thee preserve thy body and soul unto everlasting life. Take and eat this in remembrance that Christ died for thee and feed on Him in thy heart by faith with thanksgiving."[3] This was to accommodate both those who believed that communion was simply an act of remembrance and those who believed it really partook of the body of Christ. In spite of her attempts at "moderate Protestantism" she faced continued resistance from Catholics and the pope, who said they were free from any obligation of obedience to her authority. Furthermore, Mary Stuart was the queen of Scots and a devout Catholic. If Elizabeth's rule was declared illegitimate, she was next in line to the British crown. So there were many plots against Elizabeth, some of which were actually supported by Mary Stuart. Elizabeth reluctantly ordered that she be executed.

This was a time during which many Protestants in exile decided to return to England. Many of them had absorbed Calvinism while away and came home with a zeal for it. During Elizabeth's long reign, which lasted until 1603, her moderate approach began to bear fruit with Catholics beginning to make a distinction between their loyalty to the crown and the practice of their faith in loyalty to the pope. Because of that they were allowed to practice their religion openly. On the other hand, the indifference to doctrinal purity led to the rise of Calvinists who recognized a need to further purify and strengthen doctrinal standards and practice. They became known pejoratively as "Puritans."

PURITANS

We have seen demonstrated already in this and previous chapters that which is most characteristic of Calvin and Calvinists, the calling of all believers to be "word centered in faith and practice."

---

3. González, *Story of Christianity*, 2:79.

The Rise of Puritanism in England

Henry Smith, a Puritan, described it well: "We should set the Word of God always before us like a rule, and believe nothing but that which it teacheth, love nothing but that which is prescribeth, hate nothing but that which it forbiddeth, do nothing but that which it commandeth."[4] Thanks to Thomas Cranmer and Henry VIII, Holy Scripture was available to the masses and was being devoured! England was learning anew the power of God's word to show people how to live and die with the knowledge that through faith in Christ, their lives transcended both prosperity and poverty, pride and persecution. So by the time of Bloody Mary hundreds were willing to die a martyr's death because they had read the Scriptures and they knew with all their hearts and minds what Puritan John Flavel said, "The Scriptures teach us the best way of living, the noblest way of suffering, and the most comfortable way of dying."[5] Two of the three men who became known as "the Oxford martyrs"—Latimer, Ridley, and Cranmer—were burned together, and that very spot is still marked in the street of Oxford, England. Those two were Latimer and Ridley. Cranmer was also burned there, but later. Those standing nearby recorded the words of these two men facing a terrible death, tied back-to-back on the same stake. Latimer's last words to Ridley were these, "Be of good comfort, Master Ridley, and play the man. We shall this day light such a candle, by God's grace, in England, as I trust, will never be put out."[6]

JAMES I (1603–25)

Elizabeth's long reign conducting a delicate balancing act along a course of a moderate, therefore more man-centered Protestantism maintained an uneasy peace. When Elizabeth died in 1603 she had no direct heir. However, she had declared her legitimate heir to be James, son of Mary Stuart and king of Scotland. Thus he became James I of England while remaining James VI of Scotland. Since

---

4. Beeke and Reeves, *Following God Fully*, 13.
5. Beeke and Reeves, *Following God Fully*, 13.
6. Foxe, *Foxe's Book of Martyrs*, 309; Gore, "26. Edward, Mary," 32:24.

we will cover Scotland separately, for now suffice it to say that John Knox had already moved Scotland much further down the path of reformation than where England was at the time. James had been put in his place by the church leaders in Scotland, and unlike his more politically astute father, he only grudgingly worked within those constraints. Even though his mother Mary Stuart had been a strong Catholic, he was not. His true alliance was to an absolute monarchy. Therefore, he sought to maintain policies similar to Elizabeth's, what could be called "high church," the role of pomp and bishops being emphasized in worship. We saw in an earlier chapter how this form of worship has created fertile soil for authoritarian, centralized government and loss of liberties. This is what James wanted: more authority. He once said, "Without bishops, there is no king."[7] This of course didn't play well with the Puritans. Neither did the fact that he was a homosexual. Nor did they like the rulings coming from his archbishop of Canterbury, Richard Bancroft, which affirmed that episcopal hierarchy was of divine origin. These tensions only worsened when James was forced to call Parliament into session for the purpose of approving new taxes. The House of Commons was filled with many Puritans. When one of them made a passing reference to a "presbytery," James declared that there could be no closer connection between the monarchy and a presbytery than that between God and the devil.[8] The only good that came out of that session of Parliament was approval to make a new translation of the Bible, which we know as the King James Version. James was so infuriated with Parliament that he attempted to govern without it. By 1614 he was in desperate financial straits and was forced to call it into session to approve funds, hoping that the Puritans would approve if part of the funds went to support the war involving German Protestants. It was a tactic very much like we see today when Congress threatens a shutdown and loss of funding for essential activities if demand for much larger nonessential spending is not granted. He miscalculated. The Puritans in Parliament held firm, and James countered by dissolving

---

7. González, *Story of Christianity*, 2:152.
8. González, *Story of Christianity*, 2:152–53.

The Rise of Puritanism in England

Parliament. He died a few years later. These years of turbulence between the Crown and the Puritans led to an increasing interest in colonizing the New World and a period of significant migration to America. The Mayflower set sail in September of 1620. The Massachusetts Bay Company, led by John Winthrop, left in 1630.

CHARLES I (1625-49)

Charles continued the conflict with Parliament and upped the ante by appointing a very bitter opponent of the Puritans named William Laud, archbishop of Canterbury. Laud launched death warrants and orders of mutilation of Puritans. Furthermore, he turned his ire on Scotland as well. The Church of Scotland retaliated by abolishing the episcopacy and reorganizing on a Presbyterian model. This was cause for war, but Charles had no funds. So he was forced to call Parliament, which was entirely unsympathetic to his wants. He promptly dissolved it in what has forever been called "the Short Parliament." The situation continued to devolve towards civil war. While each side was organizing its forces and allies, Parliament convoked a body of theologians to advise it on theological matters. This was the Westminster Assembly from which we get the Westminster Confession of Faith and Shorter and Larger Catechisms. The hated William Laud was executed in 1644 upon order by Parliament.

OLIVER CROMWELL (1649-60)

It was about this time when Oliver Cromwell emerged on the scene. He came from a relatively wealthy family that descended from one of Henry VIII's advisors. He was a member of the House of Commons and a Puritan, but had not really stood out. He had a reputation for being an avid reader of Scripture and believed that every decision, personal or political, should be subjected to the will of God. Because of that he could be slow to arrive at a decision, but having arrived at one was unwavering at seeing it through. Once he concluded that war was inevitable and saw that the king's advantage was in cavalry, he began to assemble a small cavalry to counter it. His zeal in this effort was contagious, and soon a mighty cavalry had formed. Their conviction that they were fighting a holy war inspired them to enter battle singing hymns. It wasn't long until the entire army of Parliament was similarly inspired and unstoppable. They crushed the king's army in the Battle of Naseby and captured King Charles, who was eventually tried, condemned, and beheaded on January 30, 1649. Cromwell was offered the crown but refused it in hopes of forming a republic and was given the title "Lord Protector" instead. Before his death he named his son as his successor. The son proved not to be up to the task and resigned. This led to the restoration of the monarchy under Charles II, and the pendulum swung once again, this time back to the episcopacy, greater tolerance of Catholics, and persecution of Presbyterians. On his deathbed, to no one's great surprise, Charles II declared that he was a Catholic. Charles's brother, James II of England and the VII of Scotland, ascended the throne. His ambition was to restore Catholicism as the official religion in both kingdoms. The English rebelled and invited William, prince of Orange, and his wife Mary, James's daughter, to come and occupy the throne. This they did in 1688.

STUDY QUESTIONS

1. How does the study of the rise and fall of kings and queens help us understand the spread of Calvinism?
2. Under Henry VIII, Thomas Cranmer had the Bible translated into English and placed in all the churches of England. How might this have prepared Protestants for the persecutions that followed?

8

The Influence of Calvinism in Scotland

I said, "Let me remember my song in the night; let me meditate in my heart." Then my spirit made a diligent search: "Will the Lord spurn forever, and never again be favorable? Has his steadfast love forever ceased? Are his promises at an end for all time?" . . . You are the God who works wonders; you have made known your might among the peoples. You with your arm redeemed your people, the children of Jacob and Joseph. . . . Your way was through the sea, your path through great waters; yet your footprints were unseen. You led your people like a flock by the hand of Moses and Aaron.

Ps 77:6–8, 14–15, 19–20

SINCE AT LEAST THE time that the Romans left Britain, Scotland had been a backwater—a backward, barbarous, and savage land. As God through Moses led the Israelites out of a similar situation in Egypt, God, through John Knox, lifted the Scots from their barbarous estate to one of preeminence, ushering in the modern world.

Calvinism and the Emergence of the Modern World

Last chapter we left off with the restoration of the monarchy under Charles II, followed by James II of England and VII of Scotland. On his deathbed Charles II "came out of the closet" as a Catholic. James fully intended to restore Catholicism both in England and Scotland. The English rebelled and invited Prince William of Orange to ascend the throne, which he did in 1688. So the "see-saw" changes of pre-Cromwell days continued, and the Reformation enjoyed advances, then faced setbacks in conjunction with changes in monarchs. It was reminiscent of the days of the kings of Judah. In this chapter we look at Scotland, where God raised up another instrument to challenge the powers of the day in that land.

THE REFORMATION IN SCOTLAND

The Reformation in Scotland was perhaps more dramatic than in any other country. Theologian Loraine Boettner says, "The best way to discover the practical fruits of a system of religion is to examine a people or a country in which for generations that system has held undisputed sway."[1] I think of nations where I have lived and worked for many years. Most of the countries of South and Central America have been predominantly Roman Catholic. Though they are typically blessed by climate, and many with abundant natural resources, after hundreds of years of existence they remain among those nations characterized by corruption, poverty, and unfulfilled potential.

When I lived in Brazil, the Brazilians told this joke about themselves: The devil was arguing with God about how God was showing Brazil unfair favoritism. He said, "You have made a land with no earthquakes or hurricanes, or natural disasters. That isn't fair! It's a land blessed with abundant natural resources and a wonderful climate. Why have you given them all these advantages?" God said, "Just wait till you see the people." Another saying they have about themselves is "Brazil is the land of the future. And,

1. Boettner, *Reformed Doctrine*, 373.

The Influence of Calvinism in Scotland

it always will be." After over five hundred years from European settlement, their own citizens recognize the unfulfilled potential in places like Brazil, Argentina, Mexico, and other countries of South and Central America. Today, most are led by Communist or Socialist governments. Scotland, on the other hand, was until the twentieth century almost exclusively Calvinistic since the 1600s. McFetridge describes it prior to the arrival of Calvinism, saying, "Gross darkness covered the land and brooded like an eternal nightmare upon all the faculties of the people."[2] Another author quoted by Boettner describes the state of affairs this way: "When Calvinism reached the Scottish people, they were vassals of the Romish church, priest-ridden, ignorant, wretched, degraded in body, mind and morals."[3] Still another says they were "filthy in their persons and in their homes, poor and miserable, excessively ignorant and exceedingly superstitious."[4] Even until 1700 Scotland was Europe's poorest independent country. Yet, foundation for the transformation had been laid and this little nation would go on to reshape the world for the better. In his book *How the Scots Invented the Modern World*, Arthur Herman, who is not a Calvinist, says, "When we gaze out on a contemporary world shaped by technology, capitalism, and modern democracy, and struggle to find our own place in it, we are in effect viewing the world through the same lens as the Scots did."[5] Boettner says it is "an easy matter to pick out the one man who in the hands of Providence was the principal instrument in the reformation of Scotland. That man was John Knox. Knox made Calvinism the religion of Scotland, and Calvinism made Scotland the moral standard of the world."[6] This chapter will primarily be about Knox, but we will also look at what was going on with the monarchies of England, France, and of course Scotland.

---

2. McFetridge, *Calvinism in History*, 88.
3. Boettner, *Reformed Doctrine*, 374.
4. Boettner, *Reformed Doctrine*, 374.
5. Herman, *How the Scots Invented*, viii.
6. Boettner, *Reformed Doctrine*, 374.

MARY QUEEN OF SCOTS (MARY STUART)

Mary queen of Scots was the daughter of James V of Scotland and Mary Guise of France. Her father was killed in battle five days after her birth, making her queen of Scotland and making her mother regent.[7] At one year old her marriage to Edward VI of England, who was six, was arranged to take place once Edward reached ten years old. This was a direct threat to the Catholic Church in Scotland because Edward was being raised as a Protestant. A very powerful Scottish cardinal named Beaton had Mary kidnapped in order to prevent the marriage, and she was taken to France, where she lived in the royal court from the time she was five years old. She grew up in the finest circumstances the world had to offer at the time and became comfortable and accustomed to it. She married the dauphin[8] of France, Francis II, expecting to live her life in France. Francis died shortly after their marriage, placing her under tremendous pressure to return to Scotland, which was incomparably less comfortable and refined than France. She did not want to go, but reluctantly did in 1560. She would later come into conflict with John Knox over the role of Catholicism versus Protestantism in Scotland.

JOHN KNOX

John Knox was born on a farm along the coast of Scotland in 1510. His parents were not wealthy, but were able to pay for him to get an education at St. Andrews for the priesthood. Patrick Hamilton was a loved and respected teacher at St. Andrews and an influence to Knox in becoming Reformed in his thinking. Hamilton held private discussion groups with students, including Knox, at his home. At these, Hamilton was more open about his Reformed beliefs. The same powerful and ruthless Cardinal Beaton who had Mary queen of Scots kidnapped was at St. Andrews and sent student spies into these private discussions at Hamilton's home. One night Beaton's

---

7. As regent, she was caretaker of Scotland until her child came of age.
8. Heir apparent to the throne.

men dragged Hamilton out of bed, arrested him, and summarily burned him at the stake—all within about an hour.

Another early influence upon young Knox was George Wishart; Knox was his bodyguard for a time. Wishart was an effective and vigorous preacher of Reformed beliefs who traveled all over Scotland. During this time the small city of Dundee was affected by the plague and had been quarantined so that no one could enter or leave. They were essentially left to die. Wishart would go to the very edge of the city and preach sermons of encouragement and God's love. As the people of Scotland learned of this, love for Wishart spread along with his fame. Wishart, too, was arrested for his preaching. His prosecutor was none other than Cardinal Beaton, who had him burned at the stake. This outraged not only Protestants, but many Catholics who recognized the godly heart of Wishart, even if they disagreed with his theology. As a result, Beaton was assassinated, and Protestants took over St. Andrews. Knox was recruited to preach there. He very reluctantly agreed after much pressuring. When he began preaching, he did so with what has been described as "terrifying power." Bruce Gore says that many of today's Presbyterians would be taken aback by the white-hot preaching of the founder of our Church.[9]

The turn of events at St. Andrews did not go unnoticed by Mary Guise in France as regent of Scotland. She called for and received military support from France. St. Andrews is located along the east coast of Scotland. Ships of soldiers came from France and besieged St. Andrews, which fell in July of 1547. Knox was captured and became a galley slave on a French ship, for all practical purposes a death sentence. Slaves rowed without so much as a cover for shade. Rain or snow, winter or summer, they were exposed to the elements with little and poor-quality food, and filth to live in. This was Knox's life for nineteen months.

In later years Knox told this story from that experience: He was sitting in the galley next to his friend John Balfour. Both of them were weak, malnourished, and suffering from months of exposure to the elements. Their conversation was as follows:

9. Gore, "30. John Knox," 17:00.

Balfour: "John, do you think we will ever get out of here alive?"

Knox: "I know the Lord will deliver us. Don't forget that Satan made Joseph go into Egypt, but God meant it for good to rescue his people. Don't lose hope, brother. God is faithful. We will return to our homeland and God will give us the victory."

At that very moment they were passing St. Andrews and Balfour looked up and asked: "Look ashore, can you tell where we are?"

Knox: "Yes, I know it well, for I see the steeple of that place where God first opened my mouth in public to his glory, and I know, no matter how weak I am now, that I shall not die until I shall glorify his godly name there again."[10]

Knox's words would prove to be prophetic.

King Edward VI ascended the throne of England in 1547. Not long after, nobility sympathetic to Knox began to search for his whereabouts and finally located him. A prisoner exchange was arranged to gain his freedom in February 1549. But it was not at all certain that Knox would survive. After eight months of the best care that England could provide, he was finally strong enough to take on responsibilities, though he never fully regained his health. Around 1550 he was made court preacher, serving in that role for three years until Edward died and Bloody Mary (Mary Tudor) came to power. Of course, she began severe persecution of Protestants. Knox was able to flee England for Geneva in 1554, arriving there around the time of Servetus's execution. Calvin was very occupied at the time and this was made worse by the fallout from the execution. So he spent little time with Knox. Nevertheless, Knox absorbed a lot of Calvinism through Calvin's assistants. In 1556, he returned to Scotland and convinced nobles to enter into a covenant that was both political and theological. They became known as the Covenanters. Then in 1557 he returned to Geneva and was able to spend a great deal of time with Calvin as both

---

10. Gore. "30. John Knox," 20:39—21:52.

The Influence of Calvinism in Scotland

his student and friend. Calvin's influence upon Geneva was now having its effect so much so that Knox declared it to be "the most perfect school of Christ that ever was in the earth since the days of the Apostles."[11] The following year, 1558, Bloody Mary died and Elizabeth became queen of England, ushering in an end to the persecution of Protestants. This change in English leadership put greater pressure on the Catholic Church in Scotland and Mary Stuart increased her persecution against the Protestant "heretics," forcing them to unite. These Protestant nobles became known as "the Lords of the Congregation." They asked Knox to return to Scotland, which he did in 1558. Just as he had predicted to his friend in the galleys, Knox found himself back in Scotland and preaching at St. Andrews. His preaching was so powerful that Mary Guise, who was still serving as regent for Scotland, outlawed preaching. This caused already strained tensions to break out into what is known as the Scottish Civil War, which lasted from 1559 into 1560. Queen Elizabeth of England came to the aid of the Scottish Protestants while Mary Guise called on France to help fight the Catholic cause. As God would have it, several events took place within a short period of time that would affect the future of Scotland. Mary Stuart's husband became Francis II, king of France, and died within a few months into his reign, or about 1560. The Huguenot uprising began in France, creating a great distraction for France's continued participation in the Scottish Civil War. And Mary Stuart's mother, Mary Guise, regent of Scotland, died on June 11, 1560. So by June of 1560, the Civil War was subsiding. As a result, leadership in Scotland agreed in 1560 to accept a Scots Confession written by Knox. He had also written a *Booke of Discipline*,[12] which mapped out a vision for how politics should be done. He got most of the ideas for this from Calvin. It was revolutionary in concept in that it established a representative form of government that was accountable to the people. It did this in part by vesting power in an office, not a person. It established that offices, including the monarchy, are created by the law, i.e., *lex rex*,

11. Schaff, *Modern Christianity*, 263.
12. Knox, *First and Second Booke*.

meaning law is king. Throughout human history the reverse had been true—i.e., the monarch created the law. And these offices operating under the law are arranged in a system of checks and balances. James Madison's Federalist Paper 10 repeats what Knox had laid out over one hundred years earlier.[13]

Knox also laid out a system of universal education known as "the voice of the people in the voice of God."[14] This meant that people could be educated to be competent in matters of the state because they could read. The nobles did not like these reforms and refused to endorse the *Booke of Discipline*.

With Francis II dead, Mary Stuart found herself queen of France, queen of Scotland, and, if the original Catholic claim of the illegitimacy of Elizabeth's claim to the throne were upheld, also queen of England. Therefore, Mary Stuart was motivated to win Scotland over to Catholicism. She was very savvy about it, beginning with a charm offensive towards the Scottish nobles consisting of many French-style parties and banquets. This began to work. However, just a short distance from where these events were taking place, John Knox was holding forth with his take-no-prisoners preaching. Mary tried all her considerable repertoire of tactics to win him to her side to no avail. She tried charm. She tried intimidation. She tried compromise. She even tried crying. Knox was always the same—polite but unmoving. Knox was known as "he who feared no man." It could equally be said "no woman." But Mary feared him. She once said, "I fear the prayers of John Knox more than all the assembled armies of Europe."[15] She continued to make herself unpopular in Scotland through machinations that would favor her and the Catholic Church. Finally she was forced to abdicate the throne in 1567 and seek refuge in England under

---

13. In speaking of protections against the dangers of factions gaining power, James Madison in Federalist Paper 10 discusses the various checks and balances organized in a system of offices. Hamilton et al., *Federalist and Anti-Federalist Papers*, 20–23.

14. Gore, "30. John Knox," 16:55—17:02.

15. Gore, "30. John Knox," 18:46. See also Knox, *Collected Prayers*.

The Influence of Calvinism in Scotland

Elizabeth. She was later found guilty of conspiring against her protector and was executed.

Upon his mother Mary abdicating her throne, James VI of Scotland (later James I of England) was coronated at the age of one in 1567. Knox preached at his coronation. Just a few years later Knox preached his last sermon in 1572, the week following the St. Bartholomew's Day Massacre in France where about five thousand Protestants all over the country were killed. This horror was a topic of his sermon. Knox died in November of that same year.

His legacy to Scotland, America, and the entire world is staggering! And of course, his legacy is part of Calvin's legacy. Arthur Herman, no Calvinist, was nevertheless true to history in *How the Scots Invented the Modern World*. As such, he documented the reach of Scotland, as influenced by Knox and Calvinism, in all aspects of the birth, rise, and dominance of modern Western civilization. The impacts included banking, industry, science, education, work ethic, culture, government, and of course religion. To be sure, not all of the influential Scots were Calvinists. Some opposed Knox. But they lived, worked, and benefited from the theological, hence political, environment that was rooted in Calvinism.

Knox and Calvinism influenced some of the greatest thinking in history. For example, Adam Smith studied at Glasgow beginning in 1737 and went on to write *The Wealth of Nations*, a book that established the intellectual foundation for capitalism. Henry Home, better known as Lord Kames, along with William Robertson, created the modern study of history (before our postmodern attempts to rewrite it). This was based on an organization of human history into four stages:

1. Hunter-gatherer
2. Pastoral-nomadic
3. Agricultural
4. Commercial

Each of these stages necessitated a different level of complexity, organization, and mutual agreement around the question of property ownership. Kames in particular taught that a sense of property marked the starting point for all social arrangements. And without law serving to protect honestly acquired property, labor and industry are in vain. He argued that governments are established to "put a check on other people's avidity for our personal goods."[16] We, of course, recognize this as a duty to defend at minimum, the eighth and tenth commandments. Kames's ideas influenced not just the way history was studied, but also the practice of law and the purpose of governments.

The Scots created a universal system of education that became a model for the world. They were highly influential in the field of philosophy, producing thinkers like David Hume. Again, I am not suggesting that everything practiced or produced by the Scots was true to Calvinism. Much of it was not. What I believe is clear, though, is that Calvinism created a culture in which the gifts God granted to men could be practiced more freely. This liberty, combined with a sense of duty to God and a desire to please him, is what led to these and numerous other contributions, to the blessings and prosperity we take for granted in our modern world.

We have already seen how Knox's implementation of Calvin's ideas of government "of the people, by the people, and for the people" were at the very core of the founding of America. And America's influence on the rest of the world has been incalculable. Easily among the three most influential books used in developing the founding documents of the United States is Sam Rutherford's *Lex Rex*, meaning "the law is king." Drawing from Scripture and other classical authors, it shows that the king is not above the law, and when the king violates the law flagrantly, the people are right to resist him, even to the point of war. This was revolutionary, and something we would do well to revisit today! Against the creeping tyranny emerging in America we still hear the refrain "we the people." It hearkens back to John Knox, and Calvin before him, and has been the cry of liberty and freedom around the world for over two hundred years. It is firmly based on a faith that puts God

---

16. Herman, *How the Scots Invented*, 97.

above all things and is anchored in the first of the Ten Commandments, "You shall have no other gods before me."

Thanks to John Knox, Scotland was led out of the "wilderness" of the earthly darkness of poverty and barbarism, and out of the spiritual darkness of paganism and Catholicism. The Scots in turn would eventually lead America to throw off English tyranny in pursuit of religious liberty.

STUDY QUESTIONS

1. Prior to the establishment of Calvinism in Scotland by John Knox, what was Scotland like?
2. What were some of the defining events of John Knox's life prior to his return to Scotland in 1558?
3. What was so revolutionary about Knox's vision for government?
4. Give some examples of the Scottish influence on the emergence of the modern world.

9

The Colonial Period

> But you are a chosen race, a royal priesthood, a holy nation, a people for his own possession, that you may proclaim the excellencies of him who called you out of darkness into his marvelous light. Once you were not a people, but now you are God's people; once you had not received mercy, but now you have received mercy.
>
> —1 Pet 2:9–10

LAST CHAPTER WE LOOKED at how Calvinism and John Knox turned Scotland, one of the most backwards nations on earth, into one of the most advanced. As the Scots moved into the New World they would have a very large influence on America, and from America's influence, the world. In this chapter we pick up the story at the time of the colonization of America and how, in many cases, the motivation was to build or live in a holy nation, one in which God could be worshiped according to the dictates of conscience rather than the state. We will continue to trace God's hand working through Calvinism and Reformed denominations, especially Presbyterianism, to drive dramatic political change.

The Colonial Period

COLONIZATION

In describing the colonization of America, historian Wilfred McClay says, "In the end, English colonization was largely a private undertaking. Or rather, it was a collection of uncoordinated private undertakings, taken on by a diverse group of entrepreneurs, visionaries, and zealots, each seeking fresh opportunities of the New World for his own purposes, and each being given an extraordinary degree of freedom in pursuing those ends without being steered by a larger national vision."[1] Colonization efforts, as opposed to the migration that would come later, were organized and funded as companies. Investors owned shares in the enterprise without having to personally take part in traveling to the New World. These companies were authorized by the king of England.

JAMESTOWN

The first of these undertakings, named the Virginia Company, arrived in 1607 at Jamestown, named for James I, and was strictly a money-making enterprise. Its charter empowered it to "dig, mine, and search for all manner of mines and gold, silver, and copper."[2] It was very poorly conceived and executed. It consisted of 105 men who had come from towns and had little skill or desire for the types of manual labor required. They were employees of the company and could not own private property. So there was little incentive to work. Despite in-migration of thousands more over the years, the company muddled along, always on the verge of disaster and only kept from it by the leadership of Captain John Smith. It was finally dissolved in 1624 when Virginia became a royal colony. The ability to own private property had finally been established in the colony and had a dramatic impact on the industry of individuals. John Smith said, "When our people were fed out of the common store, and laboured jointly together, glad was he could slip from his labour, or slumber over his taske he cared not

---

1. McClay, *Land of Hope*, 23.
2. McClay, *Land of Hope*, 24.

how, nay, the most honest among them would hardly take so much true paines in a weeke, as now for themselves they will doe in a day: neither cared they for the increase, presuming that howsoever the harvest prospered, the generall store must maintain them, so that wee reaped not so much Corne from the labours of thirtie, as now three or foure doe provide for themselves."[3] Tobacco had also been discovered as a cash crop and would finally bring their long-sought prosperity, along with increasing demand for labor. This led the Virginia Company to establish a "headright" system granting land ownership following several years of indentured labor.[4]

Due to recent attempts by some to rewrite history, I want to add a brief sidenote. In 1619 (about twelve years after the Jamestown colony had been established) pirates showed up with twenty slaves they were trafficking to the Caribbean. Their ship had been blown off course. The residents of Jamestown could not pay to send the slaves back to Africa and refused to participate in the slave trade themselves, or to have them sent into slavery in the Caribbean. So with what meager funds they had, they made an offer to take the slaves as indentured servants, essentially granting them headrights. They would work for seven years to pay off the debt incurred by the colonists. In return, they would be granted their freedom at the end of those seven years. All twenty accepted the offer and stayed. Most became very successful after receiving their freedom from indentured servitude.[5]

PLYMOUTH

In contrast to Jamestown, the Plymouth Company was a religious enterprise composed of Congregationalist Calvinists. They were not technically Puritans, as Puritans remained within the Church of England with the intent of purifying it from within. Congregationalists had left the Church of England, deeming it

---

3. Smith, *Generall Historie of Virginia*, 1:222.
4. Brinkley, *Unfinished Nation*, 31.
5. Wood, *1620*, 98; Gore, "4. First American Colonies," 28:40.

The Colonial Period

hopelessly corrupted. By leaving the church, they were subjected to some forms of persecution. Therefore they left England for the Netherlands, where they spent eleven years. As their children began to pick up the language and culture of the Dutch and to lose their English heritage, their parents sought another place to raise them and to worship without persecution. Plymouth Plantation, as it was called, was established in 1620 by these "pilgrims." As they were accustomed to do in their self-governing churches, they drew up a compact, or "social contract," by which the colony would govern itself. This was called the Mayflower Compact and it explicitly states that their voyage was undertaken "for the glory of God, and advancements of the Christian faith."[6] Their leader was William Bradford.

MASSACHUSETTS BAY

The third of the three original American colonies was the Massachusetts Bay Company. It was established in 1630 and was composed of Puritans. It was also located in New England and had received its charter from King Charles I. Its leader was John Winthrop. Before making landfall, Winthrop gave a sermon that used to be standard material in history lessons across America. He said of the company, "We are entered into a covenant with God for this work.... We must consider that we shall be as a city upon a hill. The eyes of all people are upon us."[7] This language is from Jesus's Sermon on the Mount in Matt 5:14–16.

LATER COLONIES

The colony of Rhode Island was established under the leadership of the Puritan Roger Williams, who argued that no government had the right to coerce men's consciences in matters of faith. Connecticut was the most rigorously Puritan settlement in all of New

---

6. Lillback, *1599 Geneva Bible*, 1375.
7. McClay, *Land of Hope*, 27–28.

Calvinism and the Emergence of the Modern World

England.[8] The Middle Colonies of Virginia, New York, Pennsylvania, Maryland, New Jersey, and Delaware were a more diverse set than New England. Pennsylvania was founded by Quakers. Maryland was established as a refuge for Catholics, but quickly was dominated by Protestants.[9] North and South Carolina were established primarily for commercial reasons. The colony of Georgia came last in 1732, established by James Oglethorpe as a way to protect the border of the Carolina colony, address a problem of English jails, and serve as a settlement for European Protestants.[10]

The results from these colonizations were two general streams of Reformed tradition settling in roughly two geographies. The Congregationalists settled in the New England colonies. The Presbyterian Scots settled in the Middle Colonies. On the eve of the Revolutionary War there were three million people living in the American colonies. Of these, nine hundred thousand were Presbyterians of Scottish or Scots-Irish descent; six hundred thousand were Congregationalist; four hundred thousand were German or Dutch Reformed; and there were several thousand French Huguenots. Altogether almost two million of the three million people living in America were of the Reformed faith.[11] It was these people, and Presbyterians in particular, who acted with the integrity of their Calvinistic beliefs to resist tyrannical government and would eventually create a Calvinistic republic. A Calvinistic republic has two pillars: (1) *lex rex*, or law is king; and (2) authority is held in offices, not people, since people will always tend towards corruption. The Revolutionary War was declared and fought by Reformed Christians, primarily Presbyterians.

---

8. McClay, *Land of Hope*, 28.
9. McClay, *Land of Hope*, 30.
10. Coleman, *History of Georgia*, 16–17.
11. Boettner, *Reformed Doctrine*, 382; and Gore, "1. Presbyterians," 7:40.

The Colonial Period

A PRESBYTERIAN REBELLION

If you think I am overstating the role of Presbyterians and Calvinism in the Revolutionary War, consider the following. Theologian Loraine Boettner says, "Knox laid the theological foundations for the right of Christians to resist wicked rulers. Hence the American Revolution was commonly called a Presbyterian rebellion. . . . The great Revolutionary conflict which resulted in the formation of the American nation, was carried out mainly by Calvinists, many of whom had been trained in the rigidly Presbyterian college at Princeton, and this nation is their gift to all liberty loving people."[12]

For three quarters of a century, 1706–74, leading up to the time of the creation of the American republic, the Presbyterian Church was the sole example on the continent of a representative government.[13] The thirteen colonies were quite independent from each other. None of the other denominations operated across the various states in a unified way. In effect the Presbyterian Church operated as an "ecclesiastical republic." It was also the first religious body to call for the separation from England.

We see in Gillett's *History of the Presbyterian Church in the United States* the deep, sustained, whole-hearted commitment of church leaders—pastors and elders—in resisting tyrants, even with the violence of war. Gillett says, "In initiating the Revolution and sustaining the patriotic resistance of their countrymen to illegal tyranny, the ministers of the Presbyterian Church bore a conspicuous, and even foremost part. . . . They preached the duty of resisting tyrants."[14] But they did so much more than that, frightening as that might sound to today's preachers. They fought in all ranks as soldiers. Pastor John Craighead was typical. It is said of him that he fought and preached alternately. Parson James Caldwell of the Presbyterian Church of Elizabethtown, New Jersey, did all he could—word and deed, inside the church and out—to aide the cause of revolution. "In an attack upon Springfield, when

---

12. Boettner, *Reformed Doctrine*, 383–84.
13. Boettner, *Reformed Doctrine*, 385.
14. Gillett, *History of Presbyterian Church*, 1:180.

Calvinism and the Emergence of the Modern World

the wadding[15] of the patriots gave out, Caldwell ran to the Presbyterian church; and returning with his arms and pockets filled with *Watt's Psalms and Hymns*,[16] he scattered them among the soldiers, exclaiming, 'Now, boys, give them Watts!'"[17] Like many others through the ages, he paid dearly in earthly terms for putting his faith into practice. While he was away, the British shot his wife through a window of their home while she sat reading to their nine children. They then dragged her corpse into the yard and burned their home to the ground. Later in the war, Caldwell was shot and killed, leaving his nine children orphans.

As we so often read in the Psalms, we waiver when things do not go our way. We begin to doubt God's love and his power. It is just as applicable today when we look at the spreading darkness in America and the world. We have experienced setback after setback while it seems that evil just moves forward with little to slow it down, much less roll it back. This was the feeling many times during the war. After one such defeat in which General Montgomery was killed, Rev. Dr. King appealed to his listeners in a sermon that reminded them that God is not idle and he is still in control. He still loves us and takes great interest in us for our good. Then he went on to say,

> Many things, indeed, seem to be against us—a very great and powerful enemy, who have long been trained to victory; their numerous and savage allies, who, having lost their liberty, would have others in the same condition; our weakness and inexperience in war; internal enemies; the loss of many of our friends and a beloved and able general. But let not these destroy our hopes or dampen our spirits. To put too much confidence in man is the way to provoke God to deprive us of them. This may perhaps be the darkness which precedes the glorious day. . . . It is agreeable to God's method to bring low

---

15. Wadding was used in rifles to carry the bullets forward in the rifle barrel.

16. Isaac Watts wrote hymns that were popular at the time of the American Revolution.

17. Breed, *Presbyterians and the Revolution*, 59.

The Colonial Period

before he exalteth, to humble before he raises up. Let us trust in him and do our duty, and commit the event to his determination who can make these things to be for us which, by a judgment of sense, we are ready to say are against us.[18]

To say that Calvinism had a role in the American Revolution is a bit like saying Henry Ford had a role in the auto industry in America, or that Thomas Edison had a role in bringing electricity to the masses. Presbyterianism, and the Calvinism that is practiced through it, was in many ways the very basis for the Revolution. We saw earlier that it was known as a Presbyterian rebellion. Why? An explanation can be found from those same verses from which John Winthrop preached before the Massachusetts Bay Company made landfall. This same John Winthrop was a Scottish descendant of John Knox. He preached from Jesus's Sermon on the Mount to this small group who had left everything behind to live in such a way as to be salt of the earth as Jesus had told them to be: "You are the salt of the earth, but if salt has lost its taste, how shall its saltiness be restored?" (Matt 5:13). They were struggling to be as salt is, a preservative, a preservative of faith among fallen man. They also sought to be a seasoning to provide a flavor to life and enjoyment of God forever. They believed the words of Winthrop: "You are the light of the world. A city set on a hill cannot be hidden." They were men and women who expressed their faith in their actions. "Nor do people light a lamp and put it under a basket, but on a stand, and it gives light to all in the house. In the same way, let your light shine before others, so that they may see your good works and give glory to your Father who is in heaven" (Matt 5:14–15). They had a natural distrust for kings and government because those authorities tend to claim glory for themselves rather than for God. As the king tried with ever more draconian measures to force compliance, their resolve to resist only increased. In a letter to King George, one of his supporters made this observation of the Presbyterians in America: "You will have discovered that I am no friend of the Presbyterians, and that I fix all the blame of these extraordinary

---

18. Breed, *Presbyterians and the Revolution*, 64–65.

Calvinism and the Emergence of the Modern World

American proceedings upon them. Believe me sir, the Presbyterians have been the chief and principal instruments in all these flaming measures; and they always do and ever will act against government from that restless and turbulent anti-monarchial spirit which has always distinguished them everywhere when they had, or by any means could assume, power, however illegally."[19]

LEGACY AND APPLICATION

As a Presbyterian myself, that spirit has indeed been our proud legacy. Presbyterians took seriously our God-given liberty under his law. All across the colonies patriotic associations sprang up, called "the Sons of Liberty." They were also known as the "Presbyterian Junto."[20] But the rank-and-file congregant was not acting at odds with church leadership. To the contrary, it was said, "To the Presbyterian clergy the enemy felt an especial antipathy. They were accounted ringleaders of the rebellion."[21] Our Presbyterian ancestors knew they were fighting a spiritual battle and seriously equipped themselves with the whole armor of God to withstand the schemes of the devil (Eph 6:11). How well are we carrying forward that spirit of resisting those schemes? In recent years, perhaps recent decades, we have become very tolerant in the practice of our faith. We view "tolerance" as a great virtue. It can be. But then intolerance can be as well. Being intolerant of murder, theft, and bearing false witness is virtuous. It is what we are tolerant or intolerant of that matters. We seem to have forgotten that as Christians we are to be different from the world in these things, because what you tolerate depends on the authority you recognize. "No one can serve two masters, for either he will *hate* the one [that is, he will be intolerant] and love the other, or he will be devoted to the one and despise the other" (Matt 6:24; emphasis added).

---

19. Breed, *Presbyterians and the Revolution*, 37.
20. Breed, *Presbyterians and the Revolution*, 38.
21. Breed, *Presbyterians and the Revolution*, 68.

The Colonial Period

Our Presbyterian forebears understood there is an enormous difference between a "personal faith" and a King Jesus. What do I mean? Am I saying we should not have a personal faith in Christ? God forbid I say such a thing! Of course not. We need that desperately. I'm saying that is where we far too often stop. Spiritual victory cannot be won by hyper-personalizing the battle. Think about it. If our soldiers decided that "victory" meant victory for them as individuals, how many wars would we win? How many battles? We have things just backwards. We are the soldiers for Christ and his kingdom, not the reverse. Pastor Ron Kronz says, "Unfortunately, this model of hyper-personalizing spiritual engagements is bearing fruit. In exchange for so-called personal devotion, the culture of the Christian church has surrendered the world, along with its powers and principalities."[22] We hide behind the excuse of tolerance, when all too often it is tolerance of encroaching darkness. It is really a retreat that would have been foreign and shameful to our Presbyterian forebears.

When calling sinners to repentance, we often hear things like "take the log out of your own eye first." Kronz says, "Our unwillingness to call the world to repent *is* the log in our eye."[23] He says this pietistic formula for failure is as follows:

1. Never allow the bounds of Christ's rule to exceed our personal space.
2. Encourage others to pursue Christ in ways that by design never come into conflict with the world around us.
3. Find fault with and discourage the disciple of Jesus Christ who is looking to press His [God's] rights beyond their own personal experience.[24]

Our Calvinistic forebears understood this danger. They understood God is sovereign and his law reigns supreme as the liberty-giving guide for their lives: "Until heaven and earth pass

---

22. Kronz, *Fighting to Win*, 5–6.
23. Kronz, *Fighting to Win*, 6.
24. Kronz, *Fighting to Win*, 6.

Calvinism and the Emergence of the Modern World

away, not an iota, not a dot, will pass from the law until all is accomplished. Therefore whoever relaxes one of the least of these commandments and teaches others to do the same will be called least in the kingdom of heaven, but whoever does them and teaches them will be called great in the kingdom of heaven" (Matt 5:17–19). I pray that we may by God's grace be among those called great in the kingdom of heaven.

STUDY QUESTIONS

1. How influential was religion in the establishment of the initial American colonies? Explain.
2. How many people were living in the American colonies on the eve of the American Revolution, and what percent were of the Reformed faith?
3. How influential were Presbyterians in declaring and fighting the Revolutionary War?
4. How did the Presbyterian Church serve to unify the independent colonies into a commonly governed nation?
5. Is being tolerant a virtue? Why, or why not?

10

Preparing the Way for the Great Awakening[1]

Comfort, comfort my people, says your God. Speak tenderly to Jerusalem, and cry to her that her warfare is ended, that her iniquity is pardoned, that she has received from the Lord's hand double for all her sins. A voice cries: "In the wilderness prepare the way of the Lord; make straight in the desert a highway for our God. Every valley shall be lifted up, and every mountain and hill be made low; the uneven ground shall become level, and the rough places a plain. And the glory of the Lord shall be revealed, and all flesh shall see it together, for the mouth of the Lord has spoken."

—Isa 40:1–5

IN THE LAST COUPLE of chapters we have looked at how Calvinists, and primarily Presbyterians, were the single largest and most influential group supporting and fighting the Revolutionary War

---

1. Much of this chapter was inspired by Gore, "7. Precursors to Great Awakening," which was organized with a similar structure.

on the side of the Americans. In this chapter we will take a step back a bit chronologically to look at the single greatest catalyst to galvanize the separate and largely independent colonies to think of themselves as being, in a much more meaningful way, united across colonies. That catalyst was the Great Awakening. In his book *Religion and the American Mind*, Alan Heimert looks at our religious history from the Great Awakening to the Revolution. He says, "First of all, it perhaps needs to be stressed that the revival in America . . . throve on the preaching of Calvinist doctrine."[2] The Great Awakening was a culmination of preparatory work in which God had lifted up men and providentially organized events to prepare the way.

OLD LIGHTS AND NEW LIGHTS

We have seen in earlier chapters that colonization began in the 1600s. By the 1700s, colonies in America were beginning to take on a certain level of prosperity—places like Philadelphia in the Middle Colonies and Boston in New England. The descendant generations of the original colonists were reaping the benefits of their ancestors' sacrifices. They did not have firsthand experience of religious persecution. Nor had they experienced the hardships of the early colonists. They were not lacking necessities and conveniences that life in established communities provides—things like medical care; roads; markets; news from afar; skilled tradesmen like blacksmiths, coopers, millers, and many others. In other parts of the world, religious persecution and various types of discrimination were as prevalent as ever. In the 1720s things had become very difficult for Scots in Ireland. They had never been accepted by the Irish since the Scots were encouraged by the king of England to go there and farm land that had been taken by him from the Irish. The king was long gone, along with his protections allowing them to practice their faith. Many of these Scots-Irish now emigrated to America to escape these conditions. Most settled in Pennsylvania

---

2. Heimert, *Religion and American Mind*, 4.

Preparing the Way for the Great Awakening

because it was known for its religious tolerance. After they arrived they were dismayed by what they saw as a very lukewarm practice of their faith by the "comfortable Presbyterians" whose families had come to America many years prior. The newcomers and those who had been in America for generations became known as the "New Lights" and the "Old Lights," respectively. The names reflected deep-seated differences, which we will talk about even more in our next chapter.

WILLIAM TENNENT

An early example of the New Lights was a man named William Tennent. As was typical of the New Lights, he was a powerful preacher and firm believer in the need for new birth. This kind of preaching was uncomfortable for the Old Lights and he was not welcome at many of their churches. So he founded what became known as the Log College to train preachers to preach and teach this more earnest and fiery style. But his convictions were not about style. They were about substance, of which he believed the Old Lights had lost sight. William Tennent and other founders of the Log College later became trustees of the College of New Jersey, which eventually became Princeton University.[3]

GILBERT TENNENT

Another precursor to the Great Awakening, as Bruce Gore calls it, was William's son, Gilbert. Gilbert was a graduate of the Log College and had learned well. Unlike the Old Lights, who saw preaching primarily as reasoning or persuading, Gilbert believed it unleashed a supernatural power from God. His preaching would make you believe he possessed that supernatural power. He preached with awesome power and with a message that we almost never hear today—the terrible reality of eternal damnation in hell. He said, "No person ever became a true believer without first

---

3. Craven, "Log College of Neshaminy."

experiencing the terror of sin."[4] He has been called "Exhibit A of Puritan hell-fire preaching."[5] Bruce Gore says that if he preached at one of our churches today, all that would be left in the pews would be grease spots. We would just be vaporized by the power, terror, and ferocity of his preaching.[6] It is also said he would on occasion wear sackcloth like John the Baptist.[7] Again, this style of preaching was not well received by the established Old Light churches. Like his father, he, too, was frozen out of many of them. And since it never occurred to him to preach outside of a church, his impact was limited in the larger cities.

ALEXANDER CRAIGHEAD

Another little-known but still important preacher in the colonies at this time was Alexander Craighead. He was a New Light preacher who had come to Pennsylvania as a boy from Scotland. His sermons, like many New Light pastors', had unmistakable anti-British sentiment. Some British loyalists accused him of being seditious and disobedient to authority. This was a lively and ongoing debate throughout the years leading up to the Revolution. He was important for another reason too. He was a leader in the migration from Pennsylvania to North Carolina—Mecklenburg County, specifically. He was pastor of Sugaw (Sugar) Creek Presbyterian Church, which is still operating in Charlotte. He is also considered to be the spiritual father of the Mecklenburg Declaration, which was the first declaration of independence from Britain in the nation. It is obvious that Thomas Jefferson borrowed heavily from it in composing the Declaration of Independence.

---

4. Gore, "7. Precursors to Great Awakening," 14:10.
5. Gore, "7. Precursors to Great Awakening," 14:40.
6. Gore, "7. Precursors to Great Awakening," 14:50.
7. Heimert, *Religion and American Mind*, 163.

Preparing the Way for the Great Awakening

JONATHAN EDWARDS

The next person I want to look at is a more familiar name, Jonathan Edwards. He was born October 5, 1703, in East Windsor, Connecticut, to Reverend Timothy Edwards and Esther Stoddard. His father was a minister for sixty years. His mother was the daughter of the famous Reverend Solomon Stoddard of Northampton Church in Northampton, Massachusetts. It was the largest and most influential church outside of Boston. With these parents you would expect his upbringing would have provided a very strong Christian foundation, and you would be right. After finishing studies at Yale he took over as pastor at Northampton at the age of twenty-three. He was gifted with a rare intelligence, judged by historian Perry Miller to be "an intelligence as much as Emerson's, Melville's, or Mark Twain's." Miller felt that Edwards's intelligence was "both an index of American society and a comment upon it."[8] Edwards has also been described as America's first and greatest homegrown philosopher. He preached the most famous sermon in American history, "Sinners in the Hands of an Angry God," which is often misrepresented as a "hell-fire sermon" about God's wrath. Actually it is more about God's grace. It speaks to the fact that as sinners deserving of wrath, we are in God's hands and he preserves us by his grace. Jonathan Edwards was sympathetic to the New Lights, and is even called one at times. However, his preaching style was nothing like that of Gilbert or the other well-known New Light preachers. Edwards had a quiet, high-pitched voice and was nearsighted. His earlier sermons were written, so he had to hold his sermons close to his eyes to read them. You would think that this would put the congregation to sleep. It did not at all! His sermons were done so brilliantly that his congregation was riveted to his words. He left his church after serving there for twenty-five years. Later in life he became president of Princeton College, and died on March 22, 1758, from complications from a smallpox vaccination.

---

8. Jonathan Edwards Center, "Jonathan Edwards," para. 7.

Calvinism and the Emergence of the Modern World

DAVID BRAINERD

A man whose contributions to this period of our history are often forgotten is David Brainerd. I will comment a bit more on him because he is often overlooked and has a very interesting story. He was born in 1718 in Haddam, Connecticut. His father was a state legislator. His mother died when he was very young, followed by his father when David was only fourteen. He lived as an orphan in the care of an older sister. He became a Christian in 1739 at age twenty, during the time of George Whitefield's ministry. He entered Yale the same year, but was forced to leave later that year because he had contracted tuberculosis. He was able to return to Yale in the fall of 1740. Whitefield's preaching was causing divisions at Yale, with the old-guard faculty generally being against him. In 1741, the trustees issued a decree stating that if any student called the rector, a trustee, or a tutor a hypocrite, he would be expelled after the second offense. The very same day that the decree came out, Jonathan Edwards spoke at Yale's commencement address. He surprised the old guard by siding dramatically with the students. Not long afterwards in 1742, Brainerd made an unguarded remark to an acquaintance saying one of his tutors had "no more grace than a chair," and was expelled for that comment.[9] This put him in a difficult situation. His overriding calling in life was to be a missionary pastor; yet he was not ordained. It was the New Lights that finally ordained him. So he began to preach as a missionary in 1742. Over the next four years he traveled over three thousand miles on horseback and frequently in ill health due to recurrence of tuberculosis. He traveled from village to village preaching exclusively to the Native Americans. He had exactly *zero* success! He showed up time and again in village after village and was received with utter indifference. How he retained any motivation, God only knows.

Then one day he showed up at a small Delaware Indian village, exactly as he had done so many times before over the previous four years. He had absolutely no expectations that this day would be any different. But it was different! A few actually gathered to listen;

---

9. Edwards, *Works*, 1:cxvii; 2:338.

Preparing the Way for the Great Awakening

then a few more, and soon the entire village was gathered around him. They were not just politely listening either. They were hanging on every word. When he finished, they came to him in tears, tugging at his coat and pleading for him to come back![10] He did return. And a holdout, a conjurer, became converted and traveled with him to other villages. At one of the villages near the Forks of Delaware another conjurer began heckling Brainerd, even threatening to bewitch him and those with him. Brainerd describes his ex-conjurer friend confronting the heckler conjurer: "This man presently challenged him to do his worst, telling him that he himself had been as great a conjurer as he, and that notwithstanding, as soon as he felt that word in his heart which these people loved (meaning the word of God), his power of conjuring immediately left him.—And so it would you, said he, if you did but once feel it in your heart; and you have no power to hurt them nor so much as to touch one of them."[11][12]

Young Brainerd's health began failing rapidly. None other than Jonathan Edwards took him in. Edwards's daughter, Jerusha, cared for Brainerd and ultimately fell in love with him. Even with her care, he died on October 17, 1747.[13] Jerusha died four months later in February of 1748 from tuberculosis she had contracted as a result of caring for him. They are buried together in Northampton.

Brainerd's journal was published and found a wide readership.[14] It has never been out of print, and we can buy it today. He was personally responsible posthumously for the founding of both Princeton and Dartmouth Universities. Princeton was founded because of the disappointment with Yale for having expelled him. Dartmouth originated from the inspiration of educating the native population. And even Yale eventually named a building for him. It

10. Gore, "39. John Newton," 38:08.
11. Edwards, *Works*, 2:414.
12. Bruce Gore recounts the event wonderfully in his class video, "39. John Newton," 40:21.
13. Edwards, *Works*, 1:95–96.
14. Edwards, *Life and Diary*.

still stands today as the only building named after a student who had been expelled.

BEN FRANKLIN

Another of those whom Gore calls "precursors to the Great Awakening" may seem strange to make the list: Ben Franklin. Many would argue that he was not a Christian at all. I think that is inaccurate. There may well have been a period of his life in which it would have been true, but is that not true for most Christians? Bruce Gore describes there being a "young Franklin" and a "later Franklin." Franklin had grown up and prospered in America. He was the epitome of the "comfortable Presbyterian," the Old Light. He was a "just be a good person" rationalist. His favorite preacher at this time in his life was a man named Samuel Hemphill, who was so much in the "just be a good person" camp that he was eventually deposed for heresy. However, the "later Franklin" was a very different person. He was a great admirer, defender, and friend of George Whitefield. Whitefield was anything but a "just be a good person" kind of Christian. He was a Calvinist. It was the "later Franklin" who famously called for prayer when the Founding Fathers reached an impasse in drawing up the Constitution. He was the single most important promulgator of Great Awakening sermons due to his deep support for Whitefield and his influential printing business.

GEORGE WHITEFIELD

Now we come to arguably God's greatest human instrument for the Great Awakening, none other than George Whitefield.[15] If you have ever wondered how God equips his people for specific purposes, take a closer look at George Whitefield and his life. He preached to all walks of life and did so very effectively. God equipped him with

---

15. See the great two-volume biography of Whitefield by Arnold Dallimore for more on his life.

Preparing the Way for the Great Awakening

what some would consider a defect—but not Whitefield. He was cross-eyed; he had a lazy eye that wouldn't track with the other. He sometimes said in his sermons that he kept one eye on the devil and the other on God. The man was a master of masters in presenting God's word. He used humor, like the above example. He used the dramatic. He could and often did bring even hardened coal miners to tears. He was a very sincerely humble man, and his great fame never changed that. God also equipped him with incredible stamina. Over his thirty years of preaching he was constantly traveling, making thirteen trips one-way between America and Britain. In Britain he traveled all around England, Scotland, and Wales. When in America he traveled up and down the colonies from Georgia to Boston. During those many years he averaged one thousand sermons a year! Think about that. That is three sermons a day, every day, on average. Since he was always traveling and not able to preach some days, there were many days he might give five or six sermons a day. I have heard of preachers who have done this for limited periods of time. But to do this for thirty years is borderline superhuman. If this were not enough, God equipped him with a powerful voice. He occasionally preached to—and was heard by!—enormous crowds of twenty thousand or so. Ben Franklin, being the scientist that he was, could not believe this claim at first. So he tested it. One day while Whitefield was preaching, Franklin walked away from Whitefield until he could just hear him distinctly. He then calculated the area of a half-circle to that point. When he allowed two feet of space for every individual, he calculated that Whitefield could speak to thirty thousand people and be heard by all. Whitefield used these and other incredible gifts to reach as many people as he could for Christ. It is estimated that ten million people in American and Britain heard him preach. Because he was a Calvinist and therefore sympathetic to the idea of equality among men, there were churches that did not want him around. But that did not stop him. Unlike Gilbert Tennent, he did not need to preach in a church. So his reach in both Britain and the colonies was very large. It has been estimated that 80 percent of the entire population of the American colonies heard him preach at least once. More than any other person or event, it was George Whitefield and his preaching that galvanized the disparate colonies and gave them a commonality. Whitefield was known as "America's preacher." It has been said that he was the single greatest catalyst for the American Revolution, though he died before it occurred.

These were among the men who prepared the way for the Great Awakening, which took place in the 1730s and 1740s. Some, like Whitefield, were active throughout it. These and many other Calvinists were instrumental in preparing the way for the American Revolution even as they worked to disciple souls for eternity.

STUDY QUESTIONS

1. What distinguished "Old Lights" from "New Lights"?
2. Jonathan Edwards was one of the greatest minds America has produced. Tell a little about him.
3. Who was David Brainerd?
4. What role did Benjamin Franklin play in promoting Great Awakening thinking?
5. Why was George Whitefield known as America's preacher?

11

Liberty and Union under God

> And when he sits on the throne of his kingdom, he shall write for himself in a book a copy of this law ... and it shall be with him, and he shall read it all the days of his life, that he may learn to fear the Lord his God by keeping all the words of this law and these statutes, and doing them, that his heart may not be lifted up above his brothers, and that he may not turn aside from the commandment, either to the right hand or to the left so that he may continue long in his kingdom, he and his children.
>
> —Deut 17:18–20

IN CHAPTER 9 WE looked at the leading role that Calvinism played during colonial times in America and in the Revolutionary War itself. Then last chapter we stepped back in time to look at the men who prepared the way for the Great Awakening. In turn, the Great Awakening prepared the people in the colonies to fight for those truths that were held to be self-evident, as well as endowed to them by their Creator. Among them they knew to be life, liberty,

Calvinism and the Emergence of the Modern World

and the pursuit of happiness. Throughout the Great Awakening the thirteen independent colonies were also coming to think a lot about another term, "union." In his chapter we are going to look at "liberty" and "union" in particular, as well as the political influence that Calvinism had in shaping the new republic.

WHAT MAKES A NATION?

C. Greg Singer had a long and distinguished career, including his service as professor of church history and theology at the Atlanta School of Biblical Studies and Greenville Presbyterian Theological Seminary. He begins his book *A Theological Interpretation of American History* with this comment: "It is impossible to understand completely the history of a nation apart from the philosophies and the theologies which lie at the heart of its intellectual life." He goes on to say, "The great weakness in the major schools of historical interpretation of the present day lies in the fact that they have adopted either humanism, or some form of scientific naturalism, as the source of all necessary presuppositions for their philosophies of history."[1] In other words, what makes peoples who they are, are their core beliefs, their religion. This and its application to each nation's unique circumstances form the essential bases distinguishing one nation from another. Yet, religion is the very thing that is left out of most histories. Even for those nations that share a common religious heritage, like Christianity, the distinctives of that faith, such as Calvinism as opposed to Episcopalianism, or Arminianism, have enormous influence over the core beliefs of a nation. Better said, they *are* the nation's core beliefs. Those things that textbooks generally discuss to distinguish nation from nation, such as race, culture, geographic location, natural resources, GDP, population, degree of development, type of government, are all downstream from religion.

In previous chapters we saw that two thirds of Americans from the time of colonization extending at least through the

---

1. Singer, *Theological Interpretation*, 1.

Revolutionary War were Reformed Christians. Furthermore, we saw two streams of faith practice that roughly coincided with doctrinal systems: Calvinism versus less egalitarian systems that tend to be more man centered. The original colonists were largely Calvinists escaping doctrinal systems that placed men—whether priests or kings—between Christ and ordinary individuals, thereby elevating some men above others before God. Over the seventeenth and eighteenth centuries, Calvinists bifurcated into "New Lights" and "Old Lights," with the "Old Lights" taking on many of the man-centered characteristics that original colonists had fled. Of course these two doctrinal systems of God-centered Calvinism versus man-centered alternatives harken back to Gen 3:15 and the "seed of the serpent vs. the seed of the woman," without claiming either to fit perfectly. The Calvinism of the mid-to-late 1700s had been reenergized by the "New Lights" to emphasize the need for a new birth, the sovereignty of God, and a belief in the inward operation of the Holy Spirit in regeneration.[2] This form of Calvinism stood in opposition to an outwardly evolving, yet inwardly consistent man-centered faith.

TWO STREAMS OF FAITH

These two faiths were expressed in many ways. For example, they differed in their support for a revolution to break away from Britain. Historian Alan Heimert says, "The rationalist clergy were in the 1770s, nearly to a man, if not outright Tories then sympathetic to them."[3] They also placed great emphasis on social position, eloquence, and a style of preaching that demonstrated literacy and gentility. We would call it a kind of academic snobbery today. They expected a certain station in their community and that their parishioners should pay to have such a preacher so that he should not need to engage in manual labor. The Anglican minister Jonathan Boucher was very forthright about this with his Virginia

---

2. Heimert, *Religion and American Mind*, 6.
3. Heimert, *Religion and American Mind*, 17.

parishioners. He said of clergy like him, "We are often by birth, and always by education and profession gentlemen: and if the establishment of such an order of men be of moment to the welfare of society (as it unquestionably is), society is much concerned to see that the means be provided to enable us to live in a decorous and exemplary style."[4] In contrast, "The minister, according to the Calvinist, should sacrifice 'such ornaments of style as might best suit the taste of men of polite literature' in order that he might better serve 'the benefit of persons of a vulgar capacity.'"[5] And, as might be expected of two worldviews so very different, the differences extended into the meanings of words.

Heimert says, "By virtue of the disparate intellectual universes out of which the utterances of Calvinism and Liberalism emerged, the same word as employed by each often contained and communicated a quite different meaning . . . two such words were among the most important in the vocabulary of eighteenth-century Americans: 'liberty' and 'union.' Indeed, in the disparate connotations of these two words was encapsulated nearly the whole of the larger significance of the confrontation of rational and evangelical religion."[6] The more things change, the more they stay the same!

As opposed to man-centered rationalism, Calvinism is faith infused by the Holy Spirit, who applies the word in our lives. Therefore, Calvinism is to be applied to life, not confined within the walls of churches nor confined to the self-appointed mediators between God and man of the priesthood. Calvinism recognizes the condescension of God to even the lowest of society and the liberty granted by God's grace to lift up the humble with the great in an equality before God. This equality of men before a holy God has always threatened those who put themselves between God and man, or in the place of God. Let us trace the outworking of this in America.

---

4. Heimert, *Religion and American Mind*, 171.
5. Heimert, *Religion and American Mind*, 174.
6. Heimert, *Religion and American Mind*, 12.

SYSTEMS OF DOCTRINE

You will have noticed that I have already used a number of names for those opposing Calvinism: rationalists, liberals, humanists, scientific naturalists, "Old Lights." I could and will add others: Arminians, Pelagians, semi-Pelagians, Catholics, various other non-Reformed denominations, some Reformed denominations that have drifted away (such as "Old Light" Presbyterians in the 1700s and more liberal denominations today). The list is very long. You may remember from chapter 6 that A. A. Hodge argued there are only three fundamental systems of doctrine:

1. That which "denies the guilt, corruption and moral impotence of man, and makes him independent of the supernatural assistance of God." This is called Pelagianism. I think you could include atheism and humanism here.

2. Calvinism, at the opposite end of the spectrum, "emphasizes the guilt and moral impotence of man, exalts the justice and sovereignty of God, and refers salvation absolutely to the undeserved favor and new creative energy of God."

3. Lying between these two is a kind of compromise position called "Arminianism," or sometimes "semi-Pelagianism," which "admits man's original corruption, but denies his guilt; regards redemption as a compensation for innate, and consequently irresponsible, disabilities; and refers the moral restoration of the individual to the co-operation of the human with the divine energy, the determining factor being the human will."[7]

For our purposes, we will just consider Calvinism versus everything else. The reason for the many names is that man is ever searching for ways to rebel against God, thus many names are descriptors of the version of rebellion current at any given period of time.

---

7. McFetridge, *Calvinism in History*, 4.

Calvinism and the Emergence of the Modern World

"TEAMS"

Using a sports analogy you might say that the "teams" under whose banner these worldviews play change uniforms over the centuries. But their fundamental playbooks never do. Whether they wear the jersey of the Roman Empire or the Roman Catholic Church, whether they are the lords of English aristocracy, or the lords of the Washington, DC, "swamp," the basic playbook is the same: "We are the elites. And we tell everyone else how to live their lives. We call all the plays." Winning to them is creating a world in which that is possible. It is one in which not just man rules, but the most "elite" of men. Of course the circle of "elite" always narrows until there is just one ultimate ruler.

The other team has a very different playbook and a very different concept of winning. The players receive their play calls from God, not from self-appointed elites, or from monarchies, or even from themselves. Winning is not something to be achieved because it has already been achieved in Christ's victory over death and their salvation through faith in him. They play with the desire that every true artist of their game does—to achieve a mastery of their gifts for the sport. We call it "sanctification."

I use this sports analogy because teams are composed of players of differing commitments to their game plans. But they all choose on which team they are.[8] And the team places each individual in situations where they are expected to play their role. It is no different for "team Episcopalian" or "team Presbyterian." I hope this analogy is helpful as I try to explain how the playbook of Calvinism, mostly wearing the jersey of Presbyterianism, fares during the formative years of our nation. You will see that they are opposing a team that sometimes plays with the jersey of Episcopalians, other times with that of Arminians, and still other times wearing other names. Just keep in mind the two basic playbooks. If I can continue with this analogy a bit more, the two teams' playbooks

---

8. Don't mistake this for an Arminian statement. God chose the players for his team before the players chose on which team to play. The Westminster Confession of Faith speaks to this in the chapter on effectual calling. Assembly of Divines, *Westminster Confession*, 10:1–2.

also have many of the same words, but they mean very different things because they are playing two different games. For example, both teams use the words "union" and "liberty."

UNION

There was a great divide in worldview between liberals[9] and Calvinists in the decades leading up to the Revolution. Liberal clergy and parishioners placed man at the center of things. Heimert says, "Liberals derived a scheme of salvation in which time, exercise, observation, instruction and the improvement of one's original 'capacities' were the means of grace."[10] Do we not see that today? There is such an emphasis placed on "self-improvement" that it has become a religion to some. Heimert contrasts this with Calvinists. For Calvinists even scriptural truth "had to be known not merely in a doctrinal way, but by an experimental excellence which it was not reason's office to perceive and which indeed the spiritually unenlightened mind could not possibly apprehend."[11] For the Calvinist, heart knowledge, accessible only by God's grace through faith in Christ alone, gave the assurance of salvation. So the word "union" to the Calvinist referred to a union of reborn hearts that looked away from the things of this world to spiritual beauty.[12] "Set your minds on things that are above, not on things that are on earth" (Col 3:2). But this did not mean to passively wait. It did not and does not mean that Christians are to seek unity by a passive withdrawal from conflict and action. "[Jonathan] Edwards insisted that holiness 'consists not only in contemplation, and a mere passive

---

9. "Liberals" was the term used by Heimert. He defined it in terms of religion as follows: "Liberal religion for the most part accepted one of the reigning psychological postulates of the eighteenth century: that 'true happiness' results from 'the suitableness of the object enjoyed, to the faculty enjoying.'" *Religion and American Mind*, 46.
10. Heimert, *Religion and American Mind*, 46–47.
11. Heimert, *Religion and American Mind*, 45.
12. Heimert, *Religion and American Mind*, 52.

enjoyment, but very much in action.'"[13] Others erred, according to Edwards, "in conceiving their churches as sanctuaries from distress and turmoil of the world."[14] This action and engagement of the world for the Calvinist was the role that each believer had to play in bringing the kingdom of Christ into being here on earth. Although this action would of necessity often bring them into conflict, done rightly it was a means of bringing union among the saints. Edwards noted to himself with regard to this engagement of the citizens of Northampton who might be drunkards, pompous, rich, etc., "were he to condemn them too strongly, his would be the sin of pride; were he to be too courteous he would be failing the demands of his calling."[15] For Calvinists the concept of unity was "not coercion, nor hierarchy, nor a constitutional confederation united the people of God, but the mutual love of the brethren."[16]

LIBERTY

The other term on the lips of so many leading up to the Revolution was "liberty." "Liberty" to the Calvinist was liberty in Christ that freed the individual from the restrictions of status created by man and imposed by societal norms. It was as Paul described to the Colossians: "Here there is not Greek and Jew, circumcised and uncircumcised, barbarian, Scythian, slave, free; but Christ is all, and in all. . . . Whatever you do, work heartily, as for the Lord and not for men" (Col 3:11, 23). We still struggle to understand this liberty and always will apart from a saving faith in Christ. Now as then, so much of our strife and lawlessness are due to an understanding of liberty as that which frees man to pursue his own desires unrestrained by God's commands.

---

13. Heimert, *Religion and American Mind*, 110.
14. Heimert, *Religion and American Mind*, 128.
15. Heimert, *Religion and American Mind*, 139.
16. Heimert, *Religion and American Mind*, 158.

Liberty and Union under God

RISE OF DEISM

Leading up to the Revolution, the influence of Puritanism, declined and deism became more popular. Singer says, "Deism provided the motivation for not only the American Revolution, but also for the rise of democracy in America."[17] As we saw in the last chapter, "Old Light" Presbyterians were becoming less Calvinistic and more deistic in their faith as the Revolutionary period neared. Deism had been around for about 150 years, originating around 1625 from Descartes and Lord Herbert Cherbury of England. It was expressed as a drift towards so-called "rationalism." Specifically, it taught that the "knowledge of God, and what he requires of man, is rationally perceived, and the Bible is binding only to the extent to which its teachings correspond with the dictates of right reason."[18] Well, guess who determined which reason was right? Man. This is straight-up Enlightenment thinking masquerading as Christianity. But it offers what lawyers call "plausible deniability" in moving away from Christianity. "Right reason" could mean reason that rightly followed God's requirements of man. The deceiver loves these fuzzy words that can mean something that pleases God, but can just as well mean something entirely displeasing to God.

SHIFT TO ARMINIANISM AND DEMOCRACY

This concept of right reason used in combination with John Locke's idea that government exists by the consent of the people opened the door wide to democracy. "It meant the ruler was no longer responsible to God for his administration of government, but responsible to the people."[19] This fit Thomas Jefferson's taste to a *t*. And one does not have to say that people like Jefferson, Franklin, or even Locke were Deists to recognize clear steps being taken down the slippery slope away from Calvinism and towards Arminianism.

---

17. Singer, *Theological Interpretation*, 24.
18. Singer, *Theological Interpretation*, 25.
19. Singer, *Theological Interpretation*, 33.

TRANSCENDENTALISM

By the early 1800s Deism was no longer popular, except in New England. A resurgence of Evangelical Christianity, even a new awakening, was happening in the West. But in New England, Deism had been too entrenched for too long. It didn't go away. Rather it "changed its uniform" to transcendentalism. Singer says, "Transcendentalism rescued the Deism of Jefferson and his compatriots of 1776 from obscurity, it also gave to it a new form."[20] The cold rationality of Deism became a warm pantheism in which the whole universe in its totality was God. It was basically what is today called "Gaia." It also held a belief in the inherent goodness of man and the possibility of human improvement. Singer says,

> This optimism in regard to human nature, in turn, gave to Transcendentalism and the Unitarianism of the nineteenth century an unquenchable zeal for reform. . . . Their penchant for reform cannot be over-emphasized. There is little doubt that the alliance between Unitarian theology and Transcendentalism is one of the most important intellectual developments in American history, for it had profound implications on the political, social and economic history of America in that era which came to a close about 1865 . . . and the Southern reaction to these developments in the North, cannot be understood apart from their relationship to Transcendentalism.[21]

Using the analogy of teams, the "team" opposing Calvinism during Revolutionary War times was still opposing Calvinism during the time of the War between the States. The way they played the game had changed, but their objectives had not. They were still attempting to create a world in which self-anointed "elites," rather than God, ruled. This is arguably the single greatest stimulus to the War between the States, but is rarely even acknowledged. It was a religion of man, humanistic to the core. Its spokesperson was Ralph Waldo Emerson with typical expressions like this: "Let man

---

20. Singer, *Theological Interpretation*, 49.
21. Singer, *Theological Interpretation*, 49.

Liberty and Union under God

stand erect, go alone, and possess the universe."[22] As do the elites of today, they saw evil as a deficiency of proper knowledge. With their obsession for reform and their concept of evil being from a lack of proper knowledge, which of course they alone possessed, abolition became their main theater to demonstrate to the world (and to themselves) with a zeal their confident belief that for their religion of man, they were at the apex. Today we call this "virtue signaling." And like today, there was a mix of true virtue (sincere opposition to slavery) and empty, egregious, self-serving signaling. Christians who had already drifted from Calvinism were very vulnerable to this because they had already ceded much ground to a transcendentalistic philosophy. Singer says, "In the South, Old School Presbyterianism constituted a far greater majority of Presbyterianism than it did in the North, and it had much greater influence on southern thought than the Old School had in the North. As a result, there was in the South a far greater consciousness of the theological radicalism lurking behind the anti-slavery crusade, and also a much keener insight into the growing radicalism in northern thought in its many and varied implications for constitutional government, and its effect on the American way of life."[23] To be clear, being opposed to theological radicalism does not in any way mean being pro-slavery. Quite the opposite is the case. I hope that by this point it is clear that theological radicalism, being man-centric and more sympathetic to rule under "elites," is far closer ideologically to a pro-slavery stance. To properly address this would require a separate book. Suffice it to say that the vehement denial by many Southerners for 150 years that slavery was the primary cause of the War between the States is much more understandable when viewed through an egalitarian, Old School, Calvinistic lens. As a product of the South myself, this rings very true and we can see how, with the defeat of the South, this radicalism under the guise of "racial equality" is now destroying what remains of our constitutional government.

22. Singer, *Theological Interpretation*, 62.
23. Singer, *Theological Interpretation*, 82.

Calvinism and the Emergence of the Modern World

Today, we see history continuing to repeat. McFetridge says, "The same radical and implacable differences which existed between the dissenters and the Episcopalians in England continued between them on this side of the Atlantic, and finally brought them into open conflict."[24] Right up to today, where do we see the ever-widening division in America and the world? Fundamentally, is it not between the same two forces as it has always been? One side believes that liberty is something granted by man, whether it be a monarchy, a group of self-anointed "experts," or by a government that is no longer responsive to the will of the people. It demands, as in 1 Sam 8:6, "Give us a king to judge us." And in so doing, it rejects God from being king over them.

On the other side are those who believe liberty is granted by God, not for its exercise in a libertine quest for self-satisfaction. It is a grace granted that we may freely seek the fulfillment we were made for to glorify God and enjoy *him* forever. It is a liberty in which the individual submits to a sovereign God and secondarily to a government. Calvinism is a system of doctrine made for this latter form of government because when a people recognizes and willingly submits to a loving, all-powerful, and sovereign God and his law, there is no need for the use of coercive force. In submission to God they are their own king. "And when he sits on the throne of his kingdom, he shall write for himself in a book a copy of this law . . . and it shall be with him, and he shall read it all the days of his life, that he may learn to fear the Lord his God by keeping all the words of this law and these statutes, and doing them, that his heart may not be lifted up above his brothers, and that he may not turn aside from the commandment, either to the right hand or to the left so that he may continue long in his kingdom, he and his children" (Deut 17:18–20).

May we by God's grace and mercy choose to return to our heritage of a strong Calvinism and follow the one, true God, his laws, and his truth. May that resolve be renewed in us each day through the reading and hearing of his word. And in doing so, may we be a blessing to our neighbors and our nation.

---

24. McFetridge, *Calvinism in History*, 41.

STUDY QUESTIONS

1. What makes a nation a nation?
2. What are some defining characteristics of the two general streams of faith?
3. Words take on different meanings across different faith streams, or "teams." How are the words "union" and "liberty" understood in the two "teams"?
4. What was the evolution of the "team" opposed to Calvinism from Deism, to transcendentalism, to Unitarianism? Give characteristics of each.
5. More than slavery or economic exploitation, Singer argues the greatest motivation for the War between the States was at its core a struggle between Calvinistic and more man-centered worldviews. Explain his reasoning.

Bibliography

1828 Dictionary. V. 3.3. Moore Value Software, 2011–18.
Assembly of Divines. *The Westminster Confession of Faith.* Repr., Glasgow: First Presbyterian, 2001.
Bancroft, George. *History of the Colonization of the United States.* Vol. 2 of *History of the United States of America, from the Discovery of the American Continent.* 15th ed. Boston: Little, Brown, 1854.
Bavinck, Herman. *Prolegomena.* Edited by John Bolt. Translated by John Vriend. Vol. 1 of *Reformed Dogmatics.* Grand Rapids: Baker Academic, 2003.
Beeke, Joel, and Michael Reeves. *Following God Fully: An Introduction to the Puritans.* Companion book in DVD set, *Puritan: All of Life to the Glory of God.* Grand Rapids: Reformation Heritage, 2019.
Berkhoff, Louis. *Systematic Theology.* Grand Rapids: Eerdmans, 1938.
Boettner, Loraine. *The Reformed Doctrine of Predestination.* Phillipsburg, NJ: Presbyterian & Reformed, 1932.
Bonhoeffer, Dietrich. *The Cost of Discipleship.* Translated by R. H. Fuller. Revised by Irmgard Booth. New York: Simon and Schuster, 1959.
Breed, W. P. *Presbyterians and the Revolution.* Powder Springs, GA: American Vision, 2008.
Brinkley, Alan. *The Unfinished Nation: A Concise History of the American People.* 2nd ed. New York: Knopf, 1997.
Bulkeley, Craig S. *Hope for the Children of the Sun: Curing the Sonnenkinder Syndrome Called Contemporary Worship.* Black Mountain, NC: Worship, 2007.
Callaway, M. Brett. *Crossroads of the Eternal.* Eugene, OR: Resource, 2018.
———. "How Evil Advances: The Tyranny of Good Intentions." *American Thinker,* July 24, 2022. https://www.americanthinker.com/articles/2022/07/how_evil_advances_the_tyranny_of_good_intentions.html.
Carvalho, Olavo de. *O Imbecil Coletivo.* 10th ed. Campinas, Braz.: VIDE, 2021.
Chamblin, J. Knox. *Paul and the Self: Apostolic Teaching for Personal Wholeness.* Eugene, OR: Wipf & Stock, 1993.

Bibliography

Coleman, Kenneth, ed. *A History of Georgia*. 2nd ed. Athens: University of Georgia Press, 1991.
Craven, Elijah R. "The Log College of Neshaminy and Princeton University." *Journal of the Presbyterian Historical Society* 1 (1902) 308–14.
Dallimore, Arnold A. *George Whitefield*. 2 vols. Carlisle, PA: Banner of Truth Trust, 1980.
Edwards, Jonathan. *The Life and Diary of David Brainerd*. Chicago: Moody, 1980.
———. *The Works of Jonathan Edwards*. 2 vols. Repr., Peabody, MA: Hendrickson, 2003.
Foxe, John. *Foxe's Book of Martyrs*. Edited by W. Grinton Berry. Grand Rapids: Spire, 1988.
Gillett, E. H. *History of the Presbyterian Church in the United States of America*. 2 vols. Philadelphia: Presbyterian Publication Committee, 1864.
González, Justo L. *The Story of Christianity*. 2 vols. Peabody, MA: Prince, 1985.
Gore, Bruce. "1. Presbyterians and the American Revolution." YouTube, Sept. 20, 2021. https://www.youtube.com/watch?v=L9rxSyEWp2I.
———. "4. The First American Colonies." YouTube, Oct. 18, 2021. https://www.youtube.com/watch?v=nWvCpwKLdnA.
———. "7. Precursors to the Great Awakening." YouTube, Nov. 22, 2021. https://www.youtube.com/watch?v=DNNOdWwLoG4.
———. "23. The Life and Times of John Calvin (part 1)." YouTube, Jan. 16, 2014. https://www.youtube.com/watch?v=uR17M9aEnKs.
———. "26. Edward, Mary, and an English Tug-of-War." YouTube, May 20, 2014. https://www.youtube.com/watch?v=GZBjW3gLWP0.
———. "30. John Knox and a New Vision for Scotland (part 3)." YouTube, Apr. 8, 2014. https://www.youtube.com/watch?v=NAzfuLOrUEg.
———. "39. John Newton and David Brainerd." YouTube, June 29, 2014. https://www.youtube.com/watch?v=7NiwHNgtQxA.
Hamilton, Alexander, James Madison, and John Jay. *The Federalist and Anti-Federalist Papers*. Lexington, KY: Beacon Hill, 2009.
Hannula, Richard M. *Trial and Triumph. Stories from Church History*. Moscow, ID: Canon, 1999.
Heimert, Alan. *Religion and the American Mind: From the Great Awakening to the Revolution*. Cambridge: Harvard University Press, 1966.
Herman, Arthur. *How the Scots Invented the Modern World: The True Story of How Western Europe's Poorest Nation Created Our World & Everything in It*. New York: MJF, 2001.
Hervey, Tom. "On Sadness in the PCA: A Response to TE LeCroy's 'Sad Day.'" *Aquila Report*, Jan. 3, 2023. https://theaquilareport.com/on-sadness-in-the-pca-a-response-to-te-lecroys-sad-day/.
Jonathan Edwards Center at Yale University. "Jonathan Edwards: Biography." Jonathan Edwards Center, n.d. http://edwards.yale.edu/research/about-edwards/biography.

Bibliography

Knox, John. *The Collected Prayers of John Knox*. Edited by Brian G. Najapfour. Grand Rapids: Reformation Heritage, 2021.

———. *The First and Second Booke of Discipline. Together with Some Acts of the Generall Assemblies, Clearing and Confirming the Same: And an Act of Parliament*. True Covenanter, 1621. https://www.truecovenanter.com/kirkgovt/scotland_kirk_books_of_discipline_1621.phtml.

Kronz, Ron. *Fighting to Win: And Other Things I Didn't Learn in Sunday School*. N.p.: Kronz, 2020.

Lancelottt, Francis. "Jane Seymour (c. 1509–1537)." *Luminarium*, 1858. From *The Queens of England and Their Times*, 1:400–403 (New York: Appleton & Co., 1858). www.luminarium.org/encyclopedia/janeseymour.htm.

Lee, Richard G., ed. *The American Patriot Bible*. Nashville: Thomas Nelson, 2009.

Lewis, C. S. *The Abolition of Man*. New York: HarperCollins, 1974.

———. *The Screwtape Letters*. New York: HarperSanFrancisco, 1996.

Lillback, Peter A., ed. *1599 Geneva Bible*. Patriot's ed. White Hall, WV: Tolle Lege, 2010.

McClay, Wilfred M. *Land of Hope: An Invitation to the Great American Story*. New York: Encounter, 2019.

McFetridge, Nathaniel S. *Calvinism in History*. Edmonton, Can.: Still Water Revival, 1989.

McGrath, Alister E. *A Life of John Calvin*. Oxford: Blackwell, 1990.

M'Crie, Thomas. *The Life of John Knox*. ChampionsofTruthMinistry, n.d. http://www.champs-of-truth.com/reform/MCR_LKNX.PDF.

Metaxas, Eric. *Letter to the American Church*. Washington, DC: Salem, 2022.

Rand, Ayn. *The Return of the Primitive: The Anti-Industrial Revolution*. New York: Penguin, 1999.

Rushdoony, R. J. *Sovereignty*. Vallecito, CA: Chalcedon, 2007.

Rutherford, Samuel. *Lex Rex*. Colorado Springs: Portage, 2009.

Schaeffer, Francis A. *The Complete Works of Francis A. Schaeffer*. 5 vols. Wheaton, IL: Crossway, 1982.

Schaff, Philip. *Modern Christianity: The Swiss Reformation*. Vol. 8 of *History of the Christian Church*. Grand Rapids: Eerdmans, 1910.

Singer, C. Greg. *A Theological Interpretation of American History*. 3rd ed. Greenville, SC: A, 1994.

Smith, John. *The Generall Historie of Virginia, New England, and the Summer Isles with the Names of the Adventurers, Planters, and Governours from Their First Beginning An 1584 to This Present 1624*. 2 vols. Carlisle, PA: Applewood, 2006.

Smyth, Dolores. "The Four Types of Love in Scripture and How to Experience Them Today." Crosswalk, last updated June 22, 2020. https://www.crosswalk.com/faith/bible-study/agape-storge-phileo-and-eros-love-in-scripture.html.

Bibliography

Tackett, Del. "Tour 3: The Heart of God." Del Tackett, n.d. From *The Engagement Project*. https://www.deltackett.com/courses/76/engagement-project-facilitators-course/lessons/2077/tour-3-streaming.

Tzu, Sun. *The Art of War*. Translated by Lionel Giles. Repr., London: Arcturus, 2008.

Weeks, Lee. "What's Wrong with America's Pulpits?" *Decision*, Jan. 1, 2023. https://decisionmagazine.com/whats-wrong-with-americas-pulpits/.

Wood, Peter W. *1620: A Critical Response to the 1619 Project*. New York: Encounter, 2020.

Zacharias, Ravi. *The Real Face of Atheism*. Grand Rapids: Baker, 2004.

Subject Index

Abide, 5–7
Agape, 5, 7–8
Agnosticism, xii, 15
America's Preacher, 102
American Revolution/Revolutionary
    War, 41, 47, 86–87, 92–94,
    96, 102–3, 105, 109–12
Arminian/Arminianism, 17–21,
    46–47, 50, 104, 107–8, 111
Atheism, xii, 14–15

Battle of Nasely, 70
Book of Common Prayer 64,66
Booke of Discipline, 77–78
Brazil, 72–73

Conjurer, 99
COVID-19, 49
Council of Two Hundred, 52
Covenanters, 76
CRT, 55

Dartmouth, 99
Declaration of Independence, 96
Defender of the Faith, 63
Deism, 111–12,115
Dogma/Dogmatics/Dogmatism, 2,
    11–13, 16–17, 20

Enlightenment, 111

Great Awakening, 93–94, 100, 102–4

Headright, 84
Huguenots, 25, 77, 86

Institutes of the Christian Religion,
    4, 25, 28, 32–33

Jamestown, 83–84

Lex Rex, 77, 80, 86
Log College, 95
Lord Protector, 70
Lords of the Congregation, 77

Massachusetts Bay Company, 69,
    85, 89
Mayflower Compact, 85
Mecklenburg Declaration, 96
Middle Colonies, 86,94

New Lights, 94–98, 102, 105
Northampton Church, 97

Old Lights, 94–96, 100, 102, 105,
    107, 111
Oxford Martyrs, 67

Pelagianism, 46, 107
Plymouth, 84–85
Political Correctness, 2, 8

Subject Index

Postmodernism, 3
Predestination, 13–14, 16–17, 19–20
Presbyterian Church in America (PCA), 27
Presbyterian Junto, 90
Princeton, 87, 95, 97, 99
Protestant/Protestantism, 11, 23–25, 28, 59, 63, 65–67, 70, 74–77, 79, 86
Puritan/Puritanism, 43–45, 66–69, 84–85, 96

Relativism, 2–3

Short Parliament, 69
Skepticism, 2
Sons of Liberty, 90
St. Andrews, 44, 74–77
St. Bartholomew's Day Massacre, 79

Sugaw Creek Presbyterian Church, 96

Ten Commandments, 81
Totalitarianism, 48
Transcendentalism, 112–13, 115
TULIP, 14

Unitarianism, 112, 115
Universalism, 17, 20

Virginia Company, 83–84

Westminster Confession, 52, 69, 108
Westminster Shorter Catechism, 4, 69

Yale, 97–99

Name Index

Adams, John Quincy, 42
Aquinas, Thomas, iv
Augustine of Hippo, viii

Balfour, John, 75–76
Bancroft, George, 43
Bancroft, Richard, 68
Barna, George, 37–38
Bavinck, Herman, 11
Baxter, Richard, 22
Beaton, Cardinal David, 74–75
Beecher, Henry Ward, 44
Beza, Theodore, 30
Boettner, Lorraine, 16–18, 20, 72–73, 87
Boleyn, Queen Ann, 63, 65
Bonhoeffer, Dietrich, 12
Boucher, Jonathan, 105
Bradford, William, 85
Brainerd, David, 98–99, 102
Breed, W.P,. 47
Bucer, Martin, 53–54, 56
Bulkeley, Craig, 47
Bure, Idelete de, 31, 53

Caldwell, James, 87–88
Callaway, M.Brett, 2
Carvallo, Olavo de, 2
Catherine of Aragon, Queen, 62–65
Cauvin, Gerard, 22
Chamblin, Knox, 33

Charles V of Germany, King, 62, 64–65
Charles I of England, King, 47, 69–70, 85
Charles II of England, King, 70, 72
Cherbury, Lord Herbert, 111
Cop, Nicolas, 23–24
Craighead, Alexander, 96
Craighead, John, 85
Cranmer, Thomas, 62–65, 67, 70
Cromwell, Oliver 69–70

Descartes, Rene, 111

Edison, Thomas, 89
Edward VI, King, 63–64, 74–76
Edwards, Jerusha, 99
Edwards, Jonathan, 97–99, 102, 109–10
Edwards, Timothy, 97
Elizabeth, Queen, 63, 65–68, 77, 79
Emerson, Ralph Waldo, 112

Farel, William, 26, 29, 34–35, 38, 52–55
Ferdinand of Spain, King, 62
Flavel, John, 67
Ford, Henry, 89
Francis II of France, King, 74, 78
Franklin, Ben, 100–102, 111
Froude, A.J., 37, 44–46

Name Index

Gamaliel, 10-11
George of England, King, 89
Gillett, Ezra Hall, 87
Gore, Bruce, 75, 96, 100
Guise, Mary, 74-75, 77

Hamilton, Patrick, 74-75
Hancock, John, 41
Heimert, Alan, 94, 105-6, 109
Hemphill, Samuel, 100
Henry VII, King, 62
Henry VIII, King, 57, 62-64, 67, 69-70
Henry III of Orange, King William / William of Orange, 70, 72
Herman, Arthur, 73, 79
Hodge, A.A., 46, 50, 107
Hume, David, 80
Huxley, Aldous, 58

Isabella of Spain, Queen, 62

James I of England, King / James VI of Scotland, King, 67-68, 79, 83
James II of England, King / James VIII of Scotland, King, 70, 72
James V of Scotland, King, 74
Jefferson, Thomas, 96, 111-12

Kames, Lord / Home, Henry, 79-80
King, Reverend, 88
Knox, John, 57, 64, 68, 71, 73-82, 89
Kronz, Ron, 91

Latimer, Hugh, 65, 67
Laud, William, 69
Lefranc, Jeanne, 23
Leo X, Pope, 25, 53, 63
Lewis, C.S., 1, 48
Locke, John, 111
Loyola, Ignatius, 23
Luther, Martin, 4, 11-12, 22, 30, 32, 53, 63, 65

Madison, James, 78
Marguerite, Queen, 25
McClay, Wilfred, 83
McFetridge, Nathaniel, 42-46, 49, 73, 114
McGrath, Alister, 24, 57-59
Melanchthon, Philip, 31, 53-54
Metaxas, Eric, 9
Miller, Perry, 97
Montgomery, General Richard, 88
Muggeridge, Malcolm, 16-17

Nietzsche, Friedrich, 15

Oglethorpe, James, 86

Philip of Spain, King, 64

Rand, Ayn, 36
Renata of Lorraine, Duchess, 25
Ridley, Nicholas, 65, 67
Robertson, William, 79
Rushdoony, Rousas, 49
Rutherford, Samuel, 80

Sadolet, Cardinal James, 53-54
Schaeffer, Francis, 3
Schaff, Philip, 26
Servetus, Michael, 57, 59-60, 76
Seymour, Queen Jane, 63
Singer, C. Greg, 104, 111-13, 115
Smith, Adam, 79
Smith, Henry, 67
Smith, John, 83
Stoddard, Solomon, 97
Stuart, Mary / Queen of Scots, 66-68, 74, 77-79

Tandy, John, 35-36
Tennet, William, 95
Tennet, Gilbert, 95, 97, 101
Tudor, Queen Mary / Bloody Mary, 62, 64-65, 67, 76-77
Tyndale, William, 65
Tzu, Sun, 37

Name Index

Viret, Pierre, 31, 35, 54

Whitefield, George, 98, 100-102
Williams, Roger, 85
Winthrop, John, 69, 85, 89

Wishart, George, 75
Wycliff, John, 57

Zwingli, Huldrych, 11, 22, 26, 30

Scripture Index

Genesis
3:1–7   19
3:15   105
22:1   42

Deuteronomy
17:18–20   103, 114

1 Samuel
8:6   114

2 Samuel
19:8b-10   51

2 Kings
19:14–15   61

Psalms
72:19   41
72:1–2, 8, 11, 17–19   40
77:6–8, 14–15, 19–20   71
119:71   3

Proverbs
1:7   1

Isaiah
9:6   48
40:1–5   93
64:6   49

Matthew
5:13–15   89
5:14–16   85
5:17–19   91–92
6:24   90
16:25   37
28:19   4

Luke
4:10   34
4:1–13   32

John
11:33–36   7
13:34–35   8
15:8   4
15:4–11   5
17:11, 14–15, 18–23   6

Acts
5:26–30, 33–35, 38–41   10–11

Scripture Index

Romans
5:20—6:2a	29
6:1	34
8:28	19

1 Corinthians
13:1–13	8

Ephesians
1:4–7	17
6:11	90

Colossians
3:2	109
3:11,23	110

Galatians
2:5	31
5:22–23	5

1 Peter
2:9–10	82

1 John
4:8	8

www.ingramcontent.com/pod-product-compliance
Lightning Source LLC
Chambersburg PA
CBHW072150160426
43197CB00012B/2322